Jewelry Projects from a

Beading Insider

Original Designs and
Expert Advice from the
Editor of *Bead Style* Magazine

Cathy Jakicic

KALMBACH BOOKS

Kalmbach Books
21027 Crossroads Circle
Waukesha, Wisconsin 53186
www.Kalmbach.com/Books

Published in 2013
17 16 15 14 13   1 2 3 4 5

Manufactured in the United States of America

ISBN: 978-0-87116-702-6
EISBN: 978-0-87116-780-4

Editor: Karin Van Voorhees
Art Director: Lisa Bergman
Layout Designer: Kelly Katlaps
Illustrator: Kellie Jaeger
Photographers: William Zuback and James Forbes

Library of Congress Cataloging-in-Publication Data

Jakicic, Cathy.
   Jewelry projects from a beading insider : original designs and expert advice from the editor of Bead Style magazine / Cathy Jakicic.

   p. : col. ill. ; cm.

   Issued also as an ebook.
   Includes index.
   ISBN: 978-0-87116-702-6

   1. Beadwork—Patterns. 2. Beadwork—Handbooks, manuals, etc.
3. Jewelry making—Handbooks, manuals, etc. I. Title. II. Title: Beading insider

TT860 .J35 2013
745.594/2

Jewelry Projects from a

Beading Insider

Ready?

Come on inside!

I had a blast putting this book together—it's basically my dream collection of projects. The best part was rediscovering all the "aha" tips and tricks and being able to share them all in one place. In the end, it turned out to be my love letter to beading and all the beaders that have inspired me since I started at *Bead Style*.

Welcome!

So, what do you say about someone who makes jewelry and writes about it every day for a living as the editor of *Bead Style* magazine and chooses to spend the better part of a year doing the same thing during her nights and weekends? Well, you can say she was crazy—or just crazy about her job. You'd be right either way.

Calling this book *Jewelry Projects from a Beading Insider* gave me pause at first. Did that mean there are beading "outsiders"? My favorite thing about this hobby and passion is that it is so accessible to everyone. And without exception, the jewelry makers I have met are incredibly generous with their talents, friendship, and advice.

What makes a beading "insider"? In my case, I think it's luck. My position at the magazine has put me inside—in the center, actually—of an amazing world where I have been lucky enough to cross paths daily with people who have taught me nearly everything I know about creativity, inspiration, color, composition, and the perfect wrapped loop.

Every project we do for the magazine sparks ideas for two or three more projects I want to make,

and each one has taught me something about designing and making jewelry. Needless to say, I've been storing up a lot of ideas over the years and collecting dozens of tips and tidbits of knowledge about beading. I'm thrilled to be able to share them with you all in one place.

So I guess I am an insider, but the good news is that there is plenty of room on the inside. In fact, there is a spot at the beading table waiting just for you. I hope these pages will act as a road map (or a GPS?) for you to find your way to the center of a wonderful world. Learn new techniques, explore unfamiliar materials, practice your skills, and explore your creativity. I'll help you with the extra tips you need to take your hobby from a craft to a creative process. Once you've arrived, I guarantee that you'll never want to leave. You'll never run out of materials to explore, techniques to try, and new creative paths to travel.

I designed the projects in this book to cover a range of techniques and jewelry styles—I think there's something for everybody. (And if you like what you see, I can recommend a magazine I think you might like!)

Are you ready to learn? Because I'm ready to spill my secrets!

Cathy

How to Use This Book

Look for this symbol to learn **Cathy's tips**: Insider Information about techniques or materials.

Find project **materials and supply lists** on pages 86–91, and a **shopping guide** on page 91.

Use the **Index** on page 95 to quickly locate techniques, project styles, and materials.

1 See the project focus at a glance: a technique or material.

2 Step-by-step project instructions accompany the large photo.

3 Detailed step-by-step photos and instructions teach complex steps.

4 Sidebar tips tie directly to the project lesson.

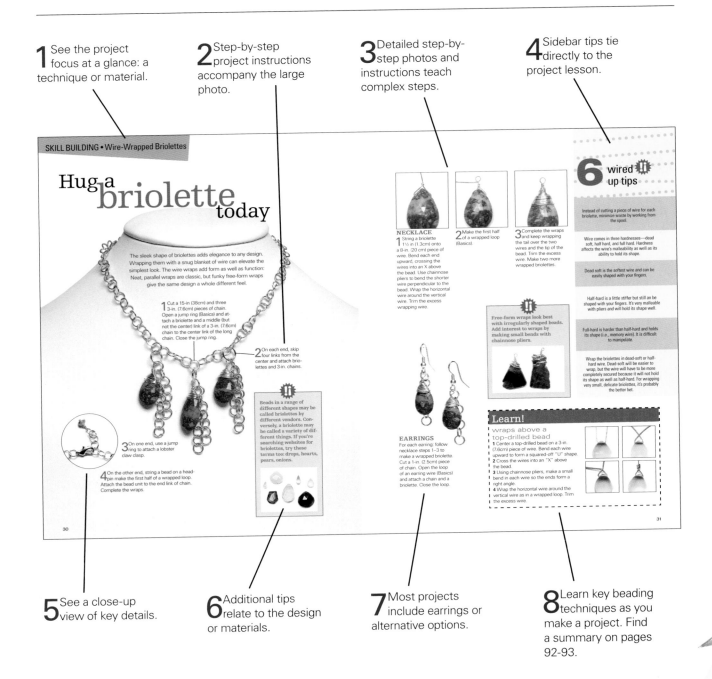

SKILL BUILDING • Wire-Wrapped Briolettes

Hug a briolette today

The sleek shape of briolettes adds elegance to any design. Wrapping them with a snug blanket of wire can elevate the simplest look. The wire wraps add form as well as function: Neat, parallel wraps are classic, but funky free-form wraps give the same design a whole different feel.

1 Cut a 15-in. (38cm) and three 3-in. (7.6cm) pieces of chain. Open a jump ring (Basics) and attach a briolette and a middle (but not the center) link of a 3-in. (7.6cm) chain to the center link of the long chain. Close the jump ring.

2 On each end, skip four links from the center and attach briolettes and 3-in. chains.

3 On one end, use a jump ring to attach a lobster claw clasp.

4 On the other end, string a bead on a head-pin make the first half of a wrapped loop. Attach the bead unit to the end link of chain. Complete the wraps.

Beads in a range of different shapes may be called briolettes by different vendors. Conversely, a briolette may be called a variety of different things. If you're searching websites for briolettes, try these terms too: drops, hearts, pears, onions.

NECKLACE
1 String a briolette 1½ in. (1.3cm) onto a 8-in. (20 cm) piece of wire. Bend each end upward, crossing the wires into an X above the bead. Use chainnose pliers to bend the shorter wire perpendicular to the bead. Wrap the horizontal wire around the vertical wire. Trim the excess wrapping wire.

2 Make the first half of a wrapped loop (Basics).

3 Complete the wraps and keep wrapping the tail over the two wires and the tip of the bead. Trim the excess wire. Make two more wrapped briolettes.

Free-form wraps look best with irregularly shaped beads. Add interest to wraps by making small bends with chainnose pliers.

EARRINGS
For each earring: follow necklace steps 1–3 to make a wrapped briolette. Cut a 1-in. (2.5cm) piece of chain. Open the loop of an earring wire (Basics) and attach a chain and a briolette. Close the loop.

6 wired up tips

Instead of cutting a piece of wire for each briolette, minimize waste by working from the spool.

Wire comes in three hardnesses—dead soft, half hard, and full hard. Hardness affects the wire's malleability as well as its ability to hold its shape.

Dead soft is the softest wire and can be easily shaped with your fingers.

Half-hard is a little stiffer but still an be shaped with your fingers. It's very malleable with pliers and will hold its shape well.

Full-hard is harder than half-hard and holds its shape (i.e., memory wire). It is difficult to manipulate.

Wrap the briolettes in dead-soft or half-hard wire. Dead-soft will be easier to wrap, but the wire will have to be more completely secured because it will not hold its shape as well as half-hard. For wrapping very small, delicate briolettes, it's probably the better bet.

Learn!

wraps above a top-drilled bead
1 Center a top-drilled bead on a 3-in. (7.6cm) piece of wire. Bend each wire upward to form a squared-off "U" shape.
2 Cross the wires into an "X" above the bead.
3 Using chainnose pliers, make a small bend in each wire so the ends form a right angle.
4 Wrap the horizontal wire around the vertical wire as in a wrapped loop. Trim the excess wire.

30

31

5 See a close-up view of key details.

6 Additional tips relate to the design or materials.

7 Most projects include earrings or alternative options.

8 Learn key beading techniques as you make a project. Find a summary on pages 92-93.

Materials

I couldn't possibly gather examples of all the beads, findings, and other materials that are available out there. Even rounding up just some of what I used in this book was a daunting task. But here are my *Beading Insider* all-star players.

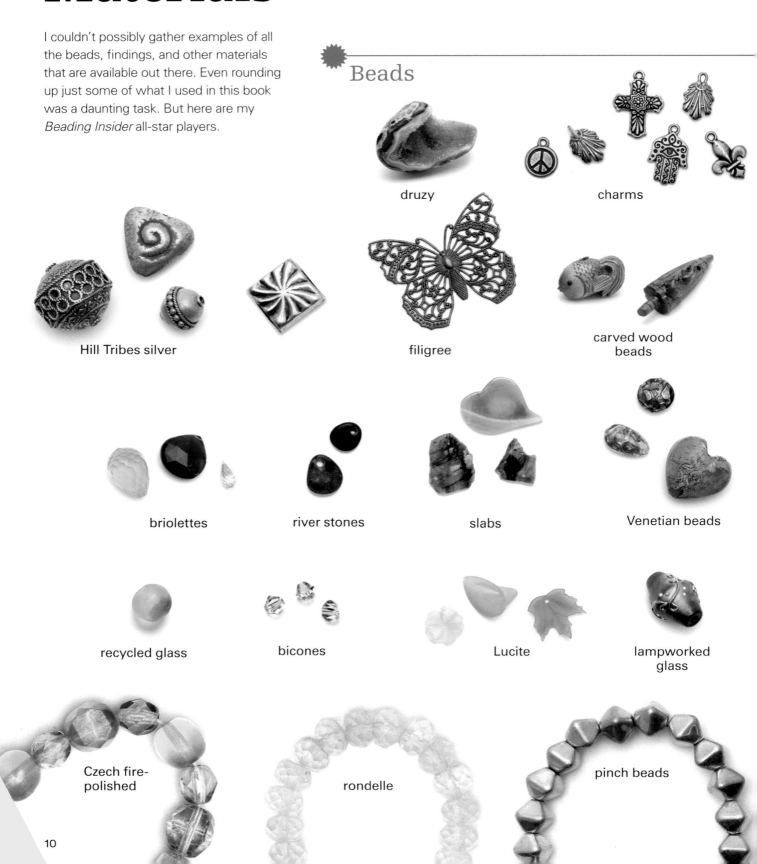

Beads

druzy

charms

Hill Tribes silver

filigree

carved wood beads

briolettes

river stones

slabs

Venetian beads

recycled glass

bicones

Lucite

lampworked glass

Czech fire-polished

rondelle

pinch beads

Stringing materials

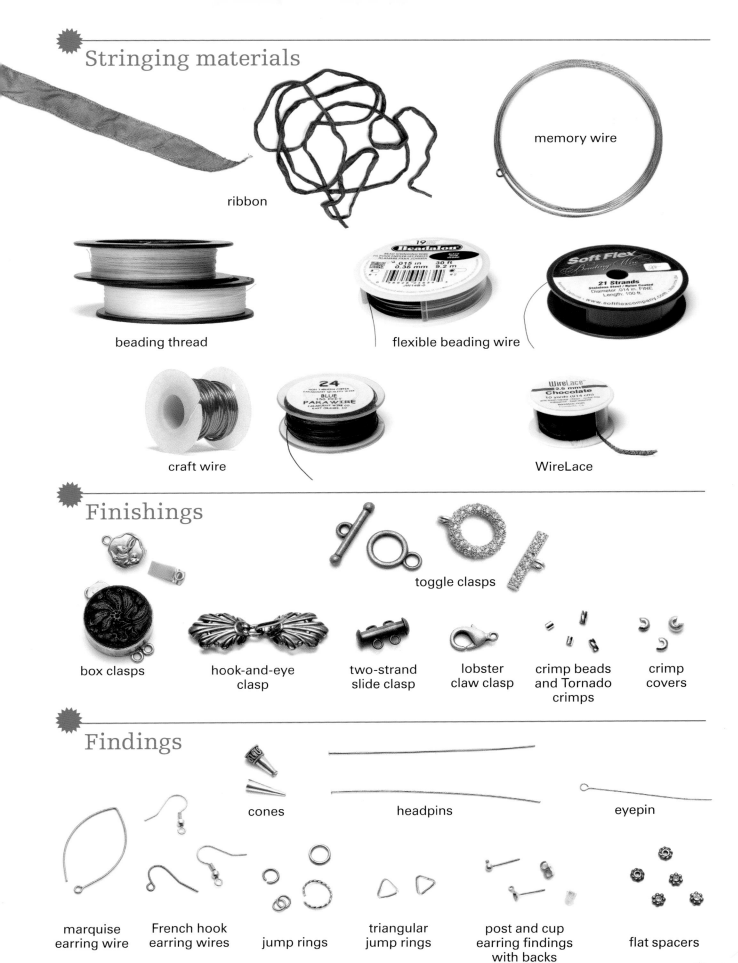

ribbon

memory wire

beading thread

flexible beading wire

craft wire

WireLace

Finishings

toggle clasps

box clasps

hook-and-eye clasp

two-strand slide clasp

lobster claw clasp

crimp beads and Tornado crimps

crimp covers

Findings

cones

headpins

eyepin

marquise earring wire

French hook earring wires

jump rings

triangular jump rings

post and cup earring findings with backs

flat spacers

Tools

One of the wonderful things about beading is that you need only a few tools to get started. So why am I showing two pages worth of goodies? Because after you start exploring and creating, there are many wonderful new things to try. Here are the tools and other helpers I used in the projects in this book.

Pliers

roundnose pliers

Adding some color

Gilders paste

metal coating

patina

clear sealant

sealant

patina

Other helpers

thread conditioner

buffer

color wheel

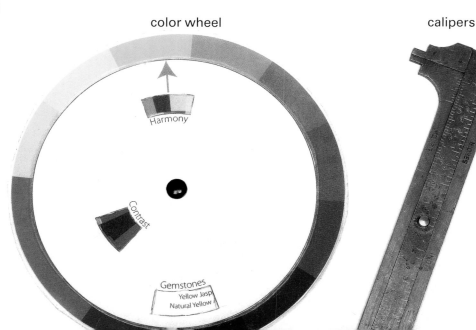

Harmony

Contrast

Gemstones
Yellow Jasp
Natural Yellow

calipers

chainnose pliers

flatnose pliers

bentnose pliers

crimping pliers

dye

hot pot

nylon-jaw pliers

hole-punch pliers

bead board

heavy-duty wire cutters

diagonal wire cutters

Skill-Building

Workshops

For these skill-building workshops, I designed projects that will let you practice some key beading techniques. Plus, you'll end up with some gorgeous jewelry while you're honing your skills!

Making wrapped and plain loops, wire wrapping, and crimping are the building blocks for most projects. And mastering these crucial skills comes with a bonus: the confidence to focus on designing.

Learning the secrets to measuring a multistrand piece, mixing colors, gilding filigree components, tackling a simple weave—even dyeing your own inexpensive glass pearls—will open more creative doors.

Learning these techniques is key, but accepting that you don't have to be perfect to make gorgeous jewelry is equally important. I've included some great tips on making stellar wrapped and plain loops, but the last thing I want to see is a quest for perfection that paralyzes the creative spirit.

This book includes all you need to learn to make jewelry you can be proud of. Perfection comes with practice, but you'll make a lot of beautiful things before you master every technique. Don't sweat it.

One exception is crimping: This one you need to nail because nobody wants a necklace that falls apart. The *Styling Your Crimps* bracelet will teach you everything you need to know.

Wrapped attention

The wrapped loop is the Swiss army knife of jewelry-making skills, so it's important to get this technique down cold. You'll use wrapped loops for everything—it's my go-to loop for most projects. They're more secure than plain loops and I actually find them easier to make and more forgiving of imperfection. This classic-with-a-twist pearl necklace has enough loops to master the technique, but not enough to overwhelm you if you're a novice.

Learn!

wrapped loop

1 Make sure you have at least 1¼ in. (3.2cm) of wire above the bead. With the tip of your chainnose pliers, grasp the wire directly above the bead. Bend the wire (above the pliers) into a right angle.
2 Using roundnose pliers, position the jaws in the bend.
3 Bring the wire over the top jaw of the roundnose pliers.

4 Reposition the pliers' lower jaw snugly into the loop. Curve the wire downward around the roundnose pliers. *This is the first half of a wrapped loop.*
5 Grasp the loop with chainnose pliers.
6 Wrap the wire tall around the wire stem, covering the stem between the loop and the top bead. Trim the excess wrapping wire and press the end close to the stem.

If you're not into the asymmetrical look, just continue the dangles all the way around.

NECKLACE

1 On a headpin, string a button pearl and a keshi pearl. Make the first half of a wrapped loop (see Learn!). Make 27 two-pearl units.

2 Cut 9 in. (23cm) of flexible beading wire. String a crimp bead, a button pearl, 2½–3 in. (6.4–7.6cm) of keshi pearls, a button pearl, and a crimp bead.

3 Cut a 4-in. (10cm) and a 15-in. (38cm) piece of chain. String an end link of each chain on one end of the pearl strand. Go back through the last beads strung. Crimp the crimp beads (p. 92) and trim the excess wire.

4 Attach a two-pearl unit to each of the first two links closest to the pearl segment. Complete the wraps.

5 Continue attaching two-pearl units, skipping a link between each unit, until the last bead unit is parallel to the top of the strung pearl segment. Check the fit and trim the chain as needed.

6 Open the jump ring (p. 92). Attach a lobster claw clasp and close the jump ring.

When first practicing wrapped loops, use 24- or 26-gauge headpins or wire. The wrapping is easier and you can concentrate on form without fighting with the wire.

Use crimping pliers to tuck in the end of the wrap.

Mark the jaw of your pliers to ensure consistent size when making multiple loops.

Make the size of the loop proportionate to the size of the bead.

If you are clustering bead units, make some stems a little longer than others so the beads have a bunched look.

Adjust the number of wraps (length of the stem) depending on how prominent you want the metal to be in your design.

Some gemstones have extremely small holes. If you're using 28-gauge wire or headpins, you can make a second set of wraps over the first for extra strength.

Take the gauge of your chain links into consideration when you choose your headpins. Here, the wrapped loop is too thick for the chain.

A two-loop bead unit has a wrapped loop on each side of the bead. Making the loops is easier if you complete the wraps on one loop before starting the other. Of course, if you need to connect the bead unit to another component with a closed loop, attach that component before you complete the wraps.

As you get more confident in your loops, you can use 1 1/2 in. (3.8cm) headpins (or less wire) to make wrapped loops. But, unless you're using sterling silver or other expensive metals, err on the side of more wire. It makes creating that elusive perfect loop much easier.

EARRINGS

For each earring: Follow necklace step 1 to make a two-pearl unit and two button pearl units. On a three-link piece of chain, attach the two-pearl unit to the bottom link and both button-pearl units to the next link. Complete the wraps. Attach the dangle to an earring wire.

Bead on a wire

For those who crochet, this is simply a chain stitch with one or two beads added with each stitch—not too much explanation necessary. But, for crochet novices, I broke it out step by step. For me, the key to creating with (and enjoying) wire crochet is embracing the irregularity. Wire is not yarn—it has a look all its own. Experiment with different wire gauges (thicknesses), hook sizes, and stitch tensions to get a range of looks. The one thing I always try to do when adding beads to the wire is to balance the size of beads to the gauge of the wire. Small beads on thicker wire look lost to me and large beads tend to make thin-wire stitches off-kilter.

BRACELET

1 On a spool of 30-gauge wire, string 8–10 in. (20–25cm) of assorted seed beads. About 6 in. (15cm) from the wire end, make a loop. Bring the 6-in. (15cm) tail behind the loop. Insert a crochet hook under the tail and over the loop.

2 Tighten the loop below the hook, leaving a little slack to form a new loop around the hook.

3 Slide one or two seed beads close to the hook. Hook the wire above the bead.

4 Bring the hook through the loop formed in step 2. This forms a new loop around the hook. Always keep the loops loose enough to bring the hook through. Repeat until the crocheted strand can circle your wrist—not too tight. Trim the wire 6 in. (15cm) from the last stitch. Make two more crocheted strands.

5 On each end of each strand, wrap the tail around the end stitch twice.

6 On each end, string a cone and a bead over all three strands. Make the first half of a wrapped loop (p. 92) with the three wires. Repeat on the other end.

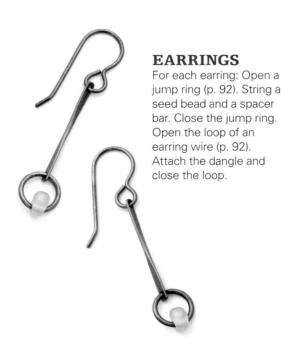

7 On each end, string one half of the clasp on the loop. Complete the wraps. Repeat on the other side.

EARRINGS

For each earring: Open a jump ring (p. 92). String a seed bead and a spacer bar. Close the jump ring. Open the loop of an earring wire (p. 92). Attach the dangle and close the loop.

6 tips for better bead crochet !!

I used 30-gauge wire for the bracelet because I couldn't resist the ethereal look, but the look comes at a price. This bracelet is very delicate and the wire will break if you are not really careful making the crochet loops.

The amount of wire needed for the bracelet varies greatly depending on the number and size of the stitches, so whenever possible, I like to work off of a spool.

If you choose not to work off of the spool, be generous when you cut the wire. Three times the desired length of the bracelet is a good length.

Before you take the time to string the beads, practice crocheting with plain wire to get a feel for the stitch size different tensions create.

This project is a great way to use your seed bead stash, but I used a color mix called "Emily's mix" by Beverly Ash Gilbert.

You can shorten the bracelet by twisting the strands together.

!! Different wire sizes craft wire, WireLace, and knitted wire

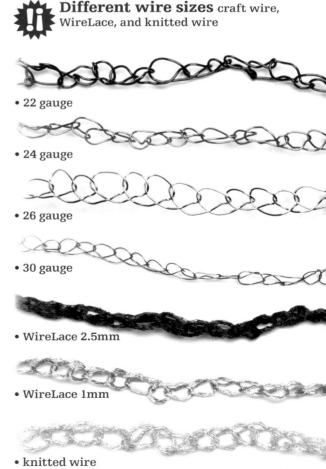

• **22 gauge**

• **24 gauge**

• **26 gauge**

• **30 gauge**

• **WireLace 2.5mm**

• **WireLace 1mm**

• **knitted wire**

19

Gild
to suit

6 On each end, open a chain link and attach half of a clasp. If your chain has soldered links, you'll need two more 4mm jump rings to attach the clasp.

I could say the reason I enjoy using Gilders paste is to add depth and a rich vintage look to brass filigree components—and it would be true. But the main reason is that I love the feel of "finger painting" the paste. Getting a rich, beautiful multilayered look is so easy—the only hard part is stopping: A little gilding goes a long way.

NECKLACE

1 Cut an 18-in. (46cm) piece of chain with a small link on each end. Center a large filigree on a large link with a jump ring (see Learn!).

2 On each end, use jump rings to attach a small, a large, and a small filigree, skipping five links between each.

5 Attach a round be[ad] unit to each sma[ll] filigree jump ring.

4 Attach a round and an oval bead unit to each large-filigree jump ring.

I chose beads that coordinated with the paste colors (olive wood and green turquoise glass), but a contrasting color (shades of violet or raspberry) will make the beads really pop.

3 Attach a round and an oval bead unit on the large links between each filigree.

Learn!

open a jump ring, loop, or link

1 Hold the jump ring, loop, or link with chainnose and roundnose pliers or two pairs of chainnose or bentnose pliers.

2 To open the jump ring, loop, or link, bring one pair of pliers toward you. Reverse the action to close.

3 gilding tips

Add touches of paste to the chain and findings to visually tie things together, but don't coat them completely.

If possible, test paste colors on extra brass components.

You can thin the paste with paint thinner if you want to use it as a stain or wash. Dried paste can be rejuvenated with paint thinner, too.

FILIGREE COMPONENTS

1 Apply Celtic bronze Gilders paste to the entire filigree (see Learn!). (This filligree was photographed before it was completely covered to illustrate the color difference.) Allow to dry about an hour between each coat.

2 Add dabs of African bronze to the entire component, but don't cover it as completely.

3 If desired, add a few highlights of the Celtic bronze. Allow to dry completely (about 12 hours) and buff with a soft cloth.

4 Use hole-punch pliers to widen the hole at the top of one petal on each flower.

BEAD UNITS

1 On a headpin, string a 4mm bead. Make a plain loop (p. 92). Make 13 round-bead and nine oval bead-units.

Learn!

gilding metal

1 Rub a small amount of paste or patina onto the metal you'd like to add color to.

2 Rub lightly with buffer. Apply sealant if you've used patina. Let dry.

EARRINGS

For each earring: Following the filigree component directions, gild a small filigree. Follow the bead unit instructions to make one round-bead and one oval-bead unit. Attach the bead units to the filigree. Use a jump ring to attach the dangle and an earring wire.

Weave
a simple sparkler

I love the immediate gratification and endless options of stringing or wirework, but sometimes I like a more challenging and meditative weaving project. If you're new to beadweaving, start with bicone crystals. They weave together nicely and offer tons of color options. If you're not up for three strands, one woven strand makes a nice tennis-style bracelet.

BRACELET

1 Cut a 24-in. (61cm) piece of beading thread. Thread a needle and condition the thread if desired. Tie on a 6º seed bead with an overhand knot, leaving an 8-in. (20cm) tail. String a 13º charlotte.

2 String two color A bicones and a charlotte.

3 Go back through the second bicone and tighten the thread.

4 Repeat steps 2 and 3 with color B.

5 Repeat steps 2 and 3 with color C.

EARRINGS

For each earring: Cut a 10-in. (25cm) piece of beading thread. Thread a needle and condition the thread if desired. Follow bracelet steps 1–5 twice. String a charlotte and go back through four or five bicones, following the thread path. Tie a half-hitch knot (p. 93). Use the 4-in. (10cm) tail to go through the loop of an earring wire. Go through four or five bicones, following the thread path. Tie a half-hitch knot.

6 Repeat steps 2–5 until the strand is the desired length. Make a second strand starting with color B and the third strand starting with color C.

7 On one end of each strand, string the loop of a three-strand clasp. Weave back through a few crystals, following the thread path, and tie a half-hitch knot (p. 93). Trim the thread. Repeat on the other end.

8 tips !! for needle & thread

Use clear 11ºs instead of the charlottes and a bold thread color so it becomes a more prominent element of your design.

Play with the order and proportion of the colors to create different patterns.

Adding or removing bicones from a woven strand is tedious; use a clasp with an extender chain to ensure a good fit.

If you can't find a clasp with the correct number of loops, clasps like this one (Jill MacKay, jillmackay.com) offer some flexibility.

The editors of *Bead&Button* magazine advise:

When threading a needle, it's easier to bring the needle to the thread. Hold the needle in your dominant hand.

Different kinds of beading needles are used for different jobs:
- #10: use with 6º–11º seed beads
- #12: use with 8º–13º seed beads
- #13: use with 11º–15º seed beads
- #16: use with 16º–24º seed beads

A small Big Eye needle is used for beadweaving and tight spots.

A twisted-wire needle is used for stringing and tight spots.

Plainly perfect

The plain loop is the strong, silent, supporting player in a jewelry deign. It has less of a visual presence than a wrapped loop, so when you have really spectacular beads—like these Venetian beauties—and you want them to be front and center, use the plain loop. The most important thing about a good plain loop is not necessarily its shape but its strength. You must make sure the loop is closed without a gap that could cause the links to separate.

2 Make five Venetian bead links and four gold bead-and-spacer links. Open one loop (p. 92) on each bead link and attach the links as shown until the strand is within 1 in. (2.5cm) of the desired length. Close the links as you go.

3 Open a loop on each end of the strand and attach one half of a clasp. Close the loops.

BRACELET

1 Cut a 2-in. (5cm) piece of wire. Make a plain loop (see Learn!). String a bead and make a plain loop. A bead with a loop on each side is a bead link.

EARRINGS

For each earring: On a headpin, string a Venetian bead. Make a plain loop. Open the loop of an earring wire. Attach a bead dangle and a round link. Close the loop.

Learn!

plain loop

1 Trim the wire ³⁄₈ in. (1cm) above the top of the bead. Make a right-angle bend close to the bead.
2 Grab the wire's tip with roundnose pliers. Roll the wire to form a half circle.
3 Reposition the pliers in the loop and continue rolling, forming a centered circle above the bead.
4 The finished loop should look like this.

Here's an alternative plain loop how-to. It's the one I prefer.

1 Make a right-angle bend close to the bead but don't trim the wire.

2 Form a loop, following the standard plain loop instructions. Use diagonal wire cutters to trim the wire just before the wire crosses over itself.

An alternative to the alternative: To make the tightest closure, trim the wire so it slightly overlaps the loop, and then use chainnose pliers to squeeze the loop so the halves are parallel.

Just between us, while the perfectly round loop is ideal, a teardrop shape will do the job just fine. If you're making a lot of small plain loops, teardrops can be easier to make and no one will know the difference.

See the wrapped loop secrets for tips on proportion and gauge (p. 17).

For larger-holed beads (like the gold ones in this bracelet), add a flat spacer on each side to make sure the plain loops snug up tightly against the bead.

Styling your. crimps

Taking the time to make a solid crimp isn't glamorous, but neither is having your jewelry fall apart. Whether you flatten or fold your crimps or go further and use wire guards and crimp covers, crimping is the one jewelry-making skill you can't fudge. Wire guards are horseshoe-shaped components that protect stringing material against fraying and wear at the point of contact with the clasp or jump ring. Crimp covers look like beads when closed and provide a pretty finish.

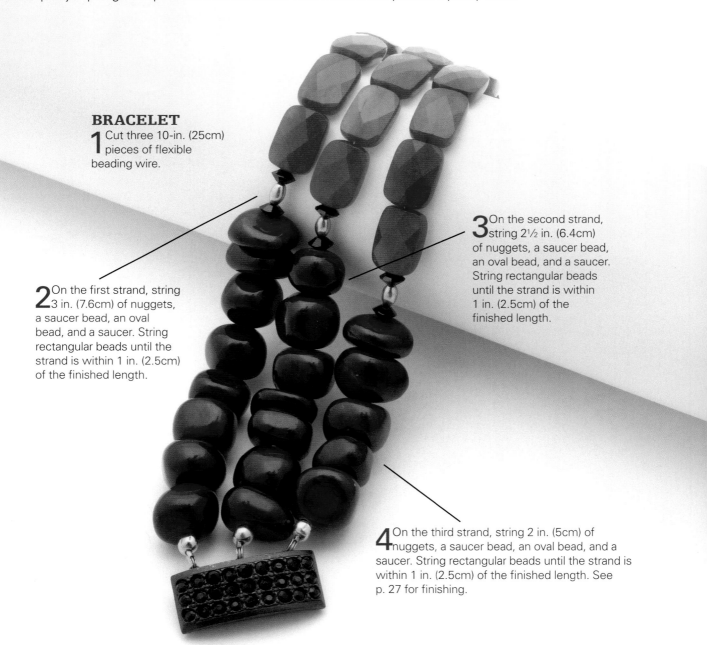

BRACELET

1 Cut three 10-in. (25cm) pieces of flexible beading wire.

2 On the first strand, string 3 in. (7.6cm) of nuggets, a saucer bead, an oval bead, and a saucer. String rectangular beads until the strand is within 1 in. (2.5cm) of the finished length.

3 On the second strand, string 2½ in. (6.4cm) of nuggets, a saucer bead, an oval bead, and a saucer. String rectangular beads until the strand is within 1 in. (2.5cm) of the finished length.

4 On the third strand, string 2 in. (5cm) of nuggets, a saucer bead, an oval bead, and a saucer. String rectangular beads until the strand is within 1 in. (2.5cm) of the finished length. See p. 27 for finishing.

Learn!

flattened crimp

1 Hold a crimp bead with the tip of your chainnose pliers. Squeeze the pliers firmly to flatten the crimp bead. Tug the clasp to make sure the crimp has a solid grip on the wire. If the wire slides, remove the flattened crimp bead and repeat with a new crimp bead.

2 The flattened crimp bead should look like this.

folded crimp

1 Position the crimp bead in the notch closest to the crimping pliers' handle.

2 Separate the wires and firmly squeeze the crimp bead.

3 Move the partially indented crimp bead into the notch at the pliers' tip. Squeeze the pliers, folding the bead in half at the indentation.

4 The folded crimp bead should look like this.

EARRINGS

On a headpin, string two nuggets and a rectangular bead. Make a wrapped loop (p. 92). Open the loop of an earring wire. Attach a dangle and close the loop. Make a second earring, reversing the number of nuggets and rectangular beads.

Most crimps are tube shaped. They are available in four sizes: 1x1 crimp beads are best with .010 and .012 beading wire; 2x2mm are used with .014 or .015; 3x3mm crimps are best used with .019 and .024; 4x4 are reserved for thicker stringing material like silk or leather cord.

Microcrimping pliers should be used with 1x1mm crimps. Mighty crimpers are best with 3x3s and 4x4s.

A twisted crimp, sometimes known as a Tornado crimp, is made with a twist in the tube that creates an indent when flattened. I used twisted crimps in the "Dream in Color" (p. 34) and "New Pearl in Town" (p. 82) projects.

For the best folded crimp, make sure that one side of the wire is on each side of the tube when you make the first squeeze.

If the notch of the crimping pliers doesn't fit around the crimp cover, use chainnose pliers (very gently) instead.

An alternative to wire guards is French wire or bullion—very thin coiled wire that is used to protect stringing material. It is strung at the same time you'd string the wire guard.

FINISHING

1 On each end of each strand, string a crimp bead and a wire guard.

2 On each end of each strand, nestle one loop of half a clasp in the corresponding wire guard. Check the fit and add or remove a rectangular bead from each strand as needed. Go back through the beads just strung. Tighten the wires and flatten the crimp beads (see Learn!). Trim the excess wire.

3 Position a crimp cover around the flattened crimp bead. Using the notch closest to the tip of your crimping pliers, gently close the cover over the crimp bead.

Lush layers

Finishing a multistrand piece with cones is an easy way to get a rich tumble of beads without worrying about the more precise measurement needed with a multistrand clasp (see the "Dyeing to Be Stylish" project on p. 32). But even with casual construction, you will need to be careful to get the most attractive drape and bead placement. The extra effort is worth it. There's nothing more striking than waves of well-composed strands. I used my favorite gemstone—labradorite—for this necklace. I accented the strands with 4mm bicone crystals in violet opal and airblue opal to highlight the flashes of color in the stones.

NECKLACE

1 Cut a 22-in. (56cm) piece of beading wire. Cut two more pieces of wire each 1 in. (2.5cm) longer than the last.

2 On each wire, string and center 12 in. (30cm) of large nuggets and bicones.

3 On each end of the shortest wire, string 2 in. (5cm) of small nuggets and bicones.

4 On each end of the middle wire, string 2½ in. (6.4cm) of small nuggets and bicones, and on each end of the longest wire, string 3 in. (7.6cm) of small nuggets and bicones.

5 Tape the ends and hold the strands together around your neck. Check the drape and add or remove beads as needed. Repeat until you have the perfect drape. Be sure to take the length of the cones and clasp into consideration. See p. 29 for finishing.

FINISHING

1 Cut a 3-in. (7.6cm) piece of 22-gauge wire. Make a wrapped loop (p. 92). On one strand, string a crimp bead and the wire loop. Go back through the crimp bead and the last beads strung. Repeat with the remaining strands. Tighten the wires and crimp the crimp beads (p. 92). Trim the excess beading wire.

2 Repeat step 1 on the other end.

3 On each end, string a cone over the wire. Make the first half of a wrapped loop.

4 On each end, attach half of a clasp and complete the wraps.

!i Arrange gemstones and bicones on a bead board to ensure the best bead placement.

!i Get the fit! If you'd like to extend the length of a necklace increasing each strand by 1 in. (2.5cm) is usually enough for shorter multistrand necklaces. For longer necklaces—matinee or longer—2–2½-in. (13–14cm) is a better increase.

EARRINGS

For each earring: On a headpin, string a bicone, a nugget, and a bicone. Make a wrapped loop. (p. 92). On a headpin, string a 4mm bicone. Make a wrapped loop. Make three bicone units. Open a loop of an earring wire (p. 92). Attach the bead and bicone units and close the loop.

Hug a briolette today

The sleek shape of briolettes adds elegance to any design. Wrapping them with a snug blanket of wire can elevate the simplest look. The wire wraps add form as well as function: Neat, parallel wraps are classic, but funky freeform wraps give the same design a whole different feel.

4 Cut a 15-in. (38cm) and three 3-in. (7.6cm) pieces of chain. Open a jump ring (p. 92) and attach a briolette and a middle (but not the center) link of a 3-in. (7.6cm) chain to the center link of the long chain. Close the jump ring.

5 On each end, skip four links from the center and use jump rings to attach briolettes and 3-in. chains.

Beads in a range of different shapes may be called briolettes by different vendors. Conversely, a briolette may be called a variety of different things. If you're searching websites for briolettes, try these terms too: drops, hearts, pears, or onions.

6 On one end, use a jump ring to attach a lobster claw clasp.

7 On the other end, string a bead on a headpin and make the first half of a wrapped loop (p. 92). Attach the bead unit to the end link of chain. Complete the wraps.

NECKLACE

1 String a briolette onto a 8-in. (20cm) piece of wire. Position the bead 1½ in. (1.3cm) from the wire end. Make a set of wraps (see Learn!) above the briolette.

2 Make the first half of a wrapped loop (p. 92) above the wraps.

3 Complete the wraps and keep wrapping the tail over the two wires and the point of the bead. Trim the excess wire. Make a total of three wrapped briolettes.

6 wired up tips

Instead of cutting a piece of wire for each briolette, minimize waste by working from the spool.

Wire comes in three hardnesses—dead soft, half hard, and full hard. Hardness relates to the wire's malleability as well as its ability to hold its shape.

Dead soft is the softest wire and can be easily shaped with your fingers.

Half-hard is a little stiffer, but still can be shaped with your fingers. It's very malleable with pliers and will hold its shape well.

Full-hard is harder than half-hard and holds its shape (e.g. memory wire). It is difficult to manipulate.

Wrap briolettes in dead-soft or half-hard wire. Dead-soft will be easier to wrap, but the wire will have to be more completely secured because it will not hold its shape as well as half-hard. For wrapping very small, delicate briolettes, soft wire is probably the better bet.

Freeform wraps look best with irregularly shaped beads. Add interest to wraps by making small bends with chainnose pliers.

EARRINGS

For each earring: Follow necklace steps 1–3 to make a wrapped briolette. Cut a 1-in. (2.5cm) piece of chain. Open the loop of an earring wire (p. 92) and attach a chain and a briolette. Close the loop.

Learn!

wraps above a top-drilled bead

1 Center a top-drilled bead on a 3-in. (7.6cm) piece of wire. Bend each wire upward to form a squared-off U shape.
2 Cross the wires into an X above the bead.
3 Using chainnose pliers, make a small bend in each wire so the ends form a right angle.
4 Wrap the horizontal wire around the vertical wire as in a wrapped loop. Trim the excess wrapping wire.

Dyeing to be stylish

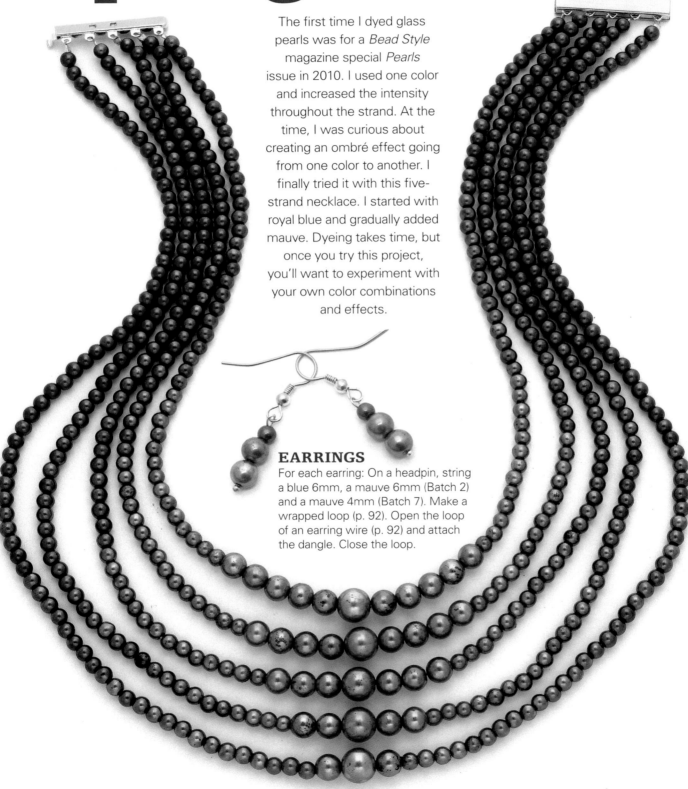

The first time I dyed glass pearls was for a *Bead Style* magazine special *Pearls* issue in 2010. I used one color and increased the intensity throughout the strand. At the time, I was curious about creating an ombré effect going from one color to another. I finally tried it with this five-strand necklace. I started with royal blue and gradually added mauve. Dyeing takes time, but once you try this project, you'll want to experiment with your own color combinations and effects.

EARRINGS

For each earring: On a headpin, string a blue 6mm, a mauve 6mm (Batch 2) and a mauve 4mm (Batch 7). Make a wrapped loop (p. 92). Open the loop of an earring wire (p. 92) and attach the dangle. Close the loop.

DYEING INSTRUCTIONS

1 Arrange your pearls on the bead board before you dye them to get the counts and positioning exactly the way you want them. Then separate and make note of each color change. Ideally, take a picture to refer to.

2 Mix dye and one tsp. vinegar in 10–12 oz. of hot (not boiling) water in a 16 oz. or larger container. Make sure the container is large enough to accommodate the pearls without overflowing. Try pint-size canning jars or 16-oz. plastic cups.

3 Keep the water hot to maintain the richness of the color. The temperature of the water makes a difference. I made a temporary double boiler from an inexpensive hot pot so I didn't need to stand by the stove all afternoon. Keep enough water in the pot to come up to about the halfway point of your container of dye.

4 Use a square of tulle (or a mesh bag) to dip your pearls. It's important to get them in and out of the dye bath all at the same time.

5 Dry pearls with a soft cloth or paper towel to minimize spots.

6 Put them back on the bead board after they are dyed (and dry) to check the effect.

TIMING

Batch 1: Dye all pearls royal blue 10 minutes, remove five 8mm, 32 6mm, and 26 4mm pearls.
Batch 2: Dip the remaining pearls in mauve for 15 seconds, remove 10 4mm and two 6mm pearls.
Batch 3: Dip the remaining pearls in mauve for 15 seconds and remove 100 4mm pearls.
Batch 4: Dip the remaining pearls in mauve for 15 seconds and remove 10 4mm pearls.
Batch 5: Dip the remaining pearls in mauve and remove 130 4mm pearls.
Batch 6: Dip the remaining pearls in mauve and remove 20 4mm pearls.
Batch 7: Dip the remaining pearls for a final 15 seconds.

4 tips to dye for !

Dye extra of the smallest pearls in case you have to adjust length, but also toss in extra in every step in case you end up with a flawed bead or you want to make an extra pair of earrings. You could always try to duplicate the color later, but that's risky because heat, timing, and who knows what else can create subtle differences in the shades.

Powder dye is more potent than liquid. Check rit.com for color formulas.

Experiment with the effects of different time and mixes before you dye the pearls for your necklace. It's well worth the extra time, and experimenting is the most fun part of the process.

The supplier of these pearls (Supplies, p. 87) sells in sets of 12 strands. Use extras for color experiments. Take good notes to refer back to later.

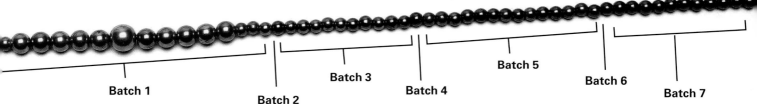

Batch 1 Batch 2 Batch 3 Batch 4 Batch 5 Batch 6 Batch 7

NECKLACE

1 Cut a 21-in. (53cm) piece of flexible beading wire. Cut four more pieces each 1 in. (2.5cm) longer than the last.

2 a. On strand 1 (15–21 in./38–53cm), center an 8mm pearl. On each end, string five 6mm pearls and two 4mm pearls from Batch 1.
b. On each end, string a 4mm from Batch 2, 10 4mms from Batch 3, a 4mm from Batch 4, 13 4mms from Batch 5, and a 4mm from Batch 6. On each end, string 4mms from Batch 7 until the strand is within ½ in. (1.3cm) of the finished length.

3 On strand 2 (16¼–22 in./41.3–56cm), center an 8mm pearl. On each end, string four 6mm pearls and three 4mm pearls from Batch 1. Repeat step 2b.

4 On strand 3 (17½–23 in./44.5–58cm), center an 8mm pearl. On each end, string three 6mm pearls and three 4mm pearls from Batch 1. Repeat step 2b.

5 On strand 4 (18¾–24 in./47.6–61cm), center an 8mm pearl. On each end, string two 6mm pearls and three 4mm pearls from Batch 1. Repeat step 2b.

6 On strand 5 (20–25 in./51–64cm), center an 8mm pearl. On each end, string a 6mm pearl and three 4mm pearls from Batch 1. Repeat step 2b.

7 On each end of each strand, string a crimp bead and the corresponding loop of half of a clasp. Check the fit and the drape of the strands and add or remove 4mms from the Batch 7 group as needed.

8 Go back through the beads just strung and tighten the wires. Crimp the crimp beads (p. 92) and trim the excess wire.

Dream in color

4 On each end, string 11ºs until the strand is within 1 in. (2.5cm) of the finished length.

No matter how clever your structural design or perfect your technique, if your colors don't work, your jewelry doesn't work. At the same time, if your color mix is brilliant (or brilliantly simple), your piece will be stunning. I love the colors of these matte Lucite petals: rich but not overpowering. I accented the predominantly cool blue with warmer teal petals to make both colors pop. Flipping the warm and cool proportions would have worked, too. Either way, always keep one color dominant.

3 On each end, string 5 in. (10cm) of beads. Alternate small and large petals with 8º and 11º seed beads. String the larger petals in pairs facing each other to add volume. After every three pairs of cool blue petals, string a pair of 30mm teal petals.

2 Over both ends, string a 15mm petal, a 30mm cool blue petal, a 15mm petal, and a cool blue, all facing down.

NECKLACE
1 Cut a 26-in. (66cm) piece of beading wire. Center a 30mm cool blue petal bead.

5 On each end, string a twisted crimp and half of a clasp. Check the fit and add or remove beads as needed. Go back through the beads just strung and tighten the wire. Flatten the crimp beads (p. 92) and trim the excess wire.

EARRINGS

For each earring:
On an open jump ring (p. 92), string a 30mm and a 15mm petal bead, both facing the same way. Close the jump ring. Open the loop of an earring wire. Attach the dangle and close the loop.

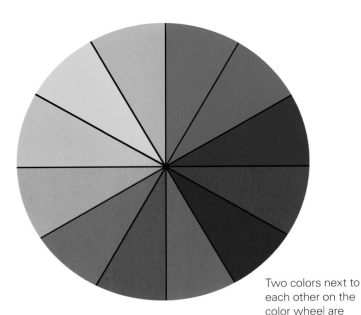

Two colors next to each other on the color wheel are called analogous and colors opposite each other are called complementary.

7 colorful tips

Two complementary colors (colors on opposite sides of the color wheel) can make each color seem more vivid. It's usually best to make one color more dominant. Even proportions can create a chaotic effect as they fight for domination.

Even in desirable proportions, true complements can come across as either too overpowering or simplistic. Using a color near the complement often gives a more pleasing, sophisticated look.

Analogous colors are next to each other on the color wheel and create a harmonious look. Mixing warm and cool tones of analogous color can create visual spice.

It's good to have a dominant color, but warm is always stronger than cool. Even in equal amounts, the warm could be more dominant.

Split complements start with one color and add two complements equally spaced on the wheel.

Double complementary (or tetradic) mixes uses four colors that are two sets of complements. Choose one color per pair to be dominant, as well as one overall.

Even neutral colors aren't completely neutral; they can lean toward warm (more red or yellow) or cool (more blue).

CREATIVITY BOOST!

We've explored the skills you need; now it's time to stretch your creative muscles. The next few projects are a bit off the beaten path, but they'll get you thinking and creating. They're a perfect trio of make-it-my-own masterpieces.

The stash project is not only a great way to use up extra beads but also it's the perfect exercise to practice mixing materials. Do you stick with one color family and mix up the shapes or will you put together a rainbow of rondelles? Either way, you'll come up with something wonderful with *Easy Stash Fashion*.

While you're trolling for hidden treasure in your bead stash, don't overlook the little things—I'm talking about seed beads. Create a colorful mosaic with a handful of beads and scraps of wire with the *Keep Costs Down, Flexibility High* bracelet. Try having a party with your beady pals and trade or pool your stashes.

The paper bracelet project is also a great one for a gathering—and definitely *Not Just for Kids*. It's a simple technique that can be a springboard for a range of great designs. Add beads or embellish the paper. Maybe it'll work with fabric—who knows? It's your world to explore.

Easy stash fashion

Most projects create leftovers—and unlike the food variety, I never throw any of them away. I toss everything in a jar and every so often, I pour out the contents in search of inspiration. There's something very satisfying about making something beautiful from your stash. It's like finding buried treasure—or a very clean $20 bill in the bottom of the washing machine. If you're like me, it's not too difficult to coordinate clusters of beads. I lean toward a certain palette in most of my jewelry, so the leftovers tend to blend together.

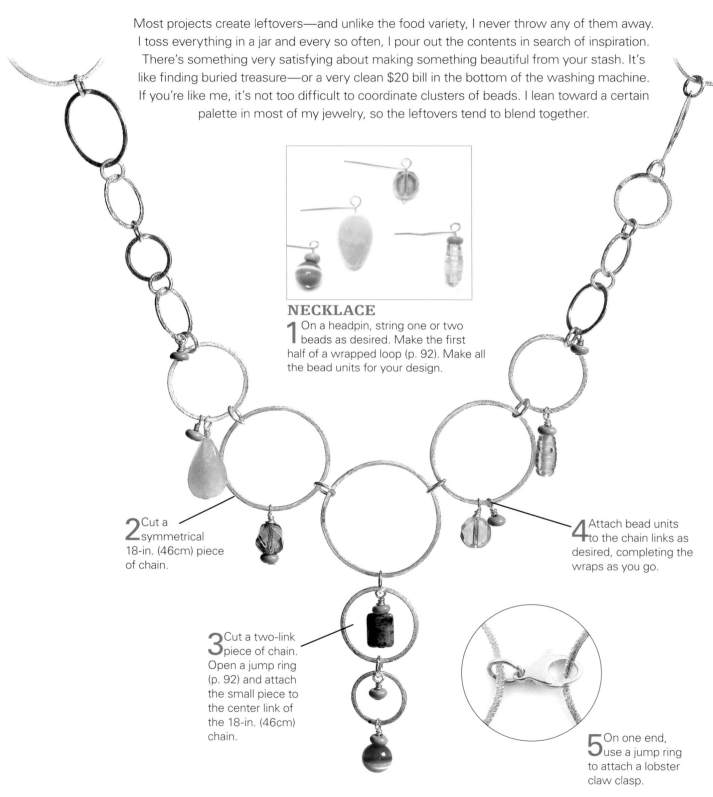

NECKLACE

1 On a headpin, string one or two beads as desired. Make the first half of a wrapped loop (p. 92). Make all the bead units for your design.

2 Cut a symmetrical 18-in. (46cm) piece of chain.

3 Cut a two-link piece of chain. Open a jump ring (p. 92) and attach the small piece to the center link of the 18-in. (46cm) chain.

4 Attach bead units to the chain links as desired, completing the wraps as you go.

5 On one end, use a jump ring to attach a lobster claw clasp.

When sorting through your beads, collect more than you'll need for the project. Then choose the beads that look best with your design.

Before making or attaching the bead units, lay your beads next to the chain and move them around until you have the best arrangement.

With this necklace, I stuck to one color family, but even if you use a more varied palette, repeating a small accent bead throughout the design will help tie it all together.

One of our designers, Linda Asperson Bergstom, gave *Bead Style* this stash tip: While you are gathering beads for one project, create "kits" of similar beads or other bead combinations for later.

large-hole pearls

EARRINGS

For each earring: On a headpin, string two beads. Make the first half of a wrapped loop (p. 92). Attach the bead unit to a link and complete the wraps. Open the loop of an earring wire (p. 92). Attach the dangle and close the loop.

Keep costs down, flexibility high

The key to making this fun, funky, extremely inexpensive bracelet is flexibility. The bracelet I ended up with isn't exactly what I expected when I started, but it turned into something I love. Being open to a bit of changing and redoing along the way and not forcing my original idea were the keys. While important to most successful designing, this attitude is particularly helpful when you're trying to stick to a budget or the materials you have on hand.

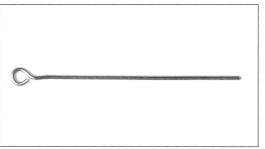

BRACELET

1 Before stringing your bracelet, plan the pattern (see p. 41). My bracelet has 15 seed beads per row. Plot the design on graph paper, or refer to a bead looming pattern for inspiration. Cut two 5-in. (13cm) pieces of small-link cable chain.

2 Cut a 1½-in. (3.7cm) piece of wire. Make a coil or plain loop at the end of the wire. Make 44–50 wire segments.

If you are using wire scraps, straighten the pieces by pulling them through the jaws of nylon-jaw pliers.

EARRINGS

For each earring: On a headpin, string nine 11º seed beads. Make the first half of a wrapped loop (p. 92). Cut a 1-in. (2.5cm) piece of chain. Attach a bead unit and complete the wraps. Open the loop of an earring wire (p. 92). Attach the dangle and close the loop.

3 On a wire segment, string the center loop of one 5-in. (13cm) chain, a row of seed beads, and the center loop of the second 5-in. chain. Make a coil or plain loop.

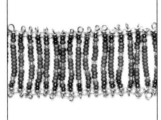

4 Continue adding rows, skipping a link between each row. If you are using coils, make sure they face the same direction.

5 Cut two ½-in. (1.3cm) pieces of chain. On the last row on each end, substitute the end link of a chain for the center seed bead. On one end, open a jump ring (p. 92) and attach a lobster claw clasp.

6 Repeat on the other end, substituting a 2-in. (5cm) piece of 5mm-link chain for the clasp. On a headpin, string nine seed beads and make the first half of a wrapped loop (p. 92). Attach the bead unit to the end of the 5mm-link chain and complete the wraps.

When you finish, go back through the rows and tighten the loops or coils. If you used plain loops, be careful that you don't pull one loop down as you are tightening the other end. You can prevent this by making sure each loop is completely closed.

4 seed bead facts

Basic seed beads have relatively large holes for their size. Japanese seed beads have a slightly square shape and are usually sold in tubes. Seed bead size is indicated by a number and the º (aught) symbol. The higher the number, the smaller the bead. Seed beads are commonly available in 15º to 6º sizes (1.5 to 4mm). Czech seed beads are more oval and are usually sold in hanks. They're also available in 15º to 6º sizes (1.3 to 4mm).

Cylinder beads are small tube beads that have thin walls and large holes. Some cylinder beads are called 11ºs, although they are actually smaller than 11º seed beads. They are sold under the brand name Delica.

Charlottes are seed beads that have a single facet that makes them sparkle. They are sometimes referred to as one-cuts or true-cuts.

Hex-cut beads have six sides and look like hexagons. They are sometimes called two-cuts. Three-cuts have additional facets on the ends to give them a softer edge.

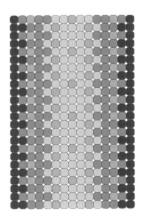

Here is the pattern I used. This represents one half of the bracelet. I used the mirror image for the other side.

Not just
for kids

When we were kids, my friends and I loved to make folded gum wrapper bracelets. I left gum wrappers (and gum) behind years ago, but the bracelet can be updated. Use fashion-forward materials such as a metal clasp, extender, and charm. Adding patina to the metal ties in with the color scheme of the paper bracelet. Even with updates, this is still a kid-friendly project.

1 Cut 14–18 1¾x4-in. (4.4x10cm) pieces of paper. Cut half in one color. Split the other half between the second and third colors. For each link: Fold the piece of paper lengthwise.

2 Open the fold. Fold each edge in to the center.

3 Fold in half lengthwise.

4 Fold the strip in half end-to-end. Fold each end in to the center. Make eight A strips, four B strips, and four C strips. The finished link will resemble a V.

5 Slide the sides of the V of a color B link into the V of a color A link.

6 Slide a color A link into the V of the second (color B) link. Keep adding links in an A-C-A-B-A-C pattern until the strand is within ½–1 in. (1.3– 2.5cm) of the circumference of your wrist.

7 Curve the bracelet to check the fit.

8 Punch a hole in each end link. On one end, open a jump ring and attach a 2-in. (5cm) chain. Close the jump ring. Use a jump ring to attach a patinated charm. On the other end, use a jump ring to attach a lobster claw clasp.

EARRINGS

For each earring: Add patina to a charm (see Learn!). With a jump ring, attach a charm to an earring wire.

5 steps to better paper folding

I experimented with different papers—fancy wrapping paper, printed scrap book paper, cardstock— before settling on the simplest, cheapest option: colored copy paper. Card-stock was too stiff, wrapping paper was too flimsy, and the patterned scrapbook paper cracked when folded.

One side of each link has more edges, the other more folds. It's easier to slide the links fold side to fold side.

Cut out a template from a heavy paper or plastic (I used a cover page from an old day planner) to keep the links uniform.

You can change the size of the links; just make sure the dimensions keep the same proportion. The width needs to be a little less than half the length. To get the right proportion, cut a piece of paper with the width at half of the length. Then trim ⅛ of the width. Use that as your template.

For more bracelet longevity, apply a spray sealant such as matte Modge Podge.

Learn! add patina

1 Rub a small amount of patina onto a charm.

2 Rub lightly with buffer and apply sealer. Let dry.

Designing

with . . .

It can be a little overwhelming. There is a virtually endless variety of beads and components available in stores and online. So now that it's all at your fingertips, what do you do? How do you turn the perfect beads into the perfect jewelry?

The projects in this section offer great ideas to get you started no matter what your favorite materials are. *Fine Facets* shows you how to make a big impact with tiny beads. *Suitable for Stringing* is just the nudge you need to do something spectacular with that art bead you splurged on and are now afraid to use. (Come on, you know you have one.)

Got some bicones? River stones? Ribbons and chain? Chunky beads? This chapter is full of ideas on making the best of them. And that's just the beginning. Mix and match designs and materials, or play with the colors. Do something that makes the projects uniquely you.

You can also explore the best way to use your favorite metal. Whether you are a gold lover or a silver fan, you'll learn to make either shine. I especially like copper jewelry. Who says jewelry has to be expensive to be spectacular?

Fine facets

Gemstones don't have to be big to make an impact. Small stones offer a subtler statement, but they have timeless style and are easy to wear. Your gemstone choice depends on your taste and budget—this design works with any stone (or for that matter, any small crystal or bead)—just keep the dimensions tiny.

Here, fine chain balances the delicate dangles. One challenge with using fine chain is that it requires equally fine jump rings—which, honestly, can make me nervous. Instead, I used bead units as connectors. They are more secure and completely work with the design. (The photo is enlarged so you can see the detail.)

5 On one end, use a bead unit to attach the soldered jump ring. On the other end, use a bead unit to attach a clasp.

4 Skip a link and use a bead unit to attach the 8-in. (20cm) chain.

NECKLACE

1 On a headpin, string a 4mm rondelle. Make the first half of a wrapped loop (p. 92). Make a total of 15 bead units.

2 Cut a 10-in. (25cm) and an 8-in. (20cm) piece of chain.

3 On the longer chain, attach a bead unit to the end link and complete the wraps. Skipping a link between each, attach 11 more bead units.

!i **Clean soft stones** with a soft cloth. You can use a soft brush on harder stones. Use warm (never hot or boiling) mild-soapy water. Amethyst, emerald, pearl, peridot, opal, tanzanite, and jade are soft stones. Garnet, aquamarine, diamond, ruby, sapphire, citrine, and topaz are harder stones.

EARRINGS

For each earring: Cut a ½-in. (1.3cm) piece of chain. On a headpin, string a 4mm rondelle. Make the first half of a wrapped loop (p. 92). Make a total of five bead units. Attach a bead unit to the end link and complete the wraps. Skipping a link between each, attach three more bead units. Use a bead unit to attach the dangle to the loop of an earring wire.

!i **For most small gemstones,** you'll need very fine-gauge headpins. It's often difficult to find headpins finer than 26 gauge, but lately I've seen 28-gauge pins on etsy.com and some 14k gold 30-gauge pins at Fire Mountain Gems and Beads, firemountaingems.com.

7 !i gemstone shopping tips

Gemstone beads can be sold individually or on strands. High-quality stones may be sold in 8-in. (20cm) or shorter strands, separated by plastic or wire spacers. These strands are often sold by weight. Other gemstones are sold in 16-in. (41cm) strands.

Highly faceted gemstones are more pricey because of the extra work of cutting and polishing the stones.

Most commercially available gemstone beads have been enhanced. Enhancements include dyeing, irradiation, heat treatment, and stabilizing with resin or wax. These treatments improve the appearance or durability of a gemstone. Not all treatments are permanent, so ask the vendor if you have questions.

As a general rule, gemstones with deep, consistent color and few inclusions (fissures or spots) are more valuable.

These last three tips are from Irina Miech, author, designer, and owner of Eclectica, a bead shop in Brookfield, Wisc.:

Check that holes are consistently drilled without jagged edges.

If the stones are strung on similarly colored string, they've probably been dyed. If possible, bring a damp light-colored cloth with you to check colorfastness.

Examine strands carefully before you buy. All gemstones are not alike; look for chips, uniformity of size and shape, inclusions, and other possible flaws.

Nurture a natural wonder

While I've always admired the understated elegance of natural materials like these smooth river stones, I couldn't resist adding a little more color and texture to the chain and findings with Swellegant copper metal coating and verdigris patina. I liked the results so much I used the coatings to create a mossy effect on the stones as well.

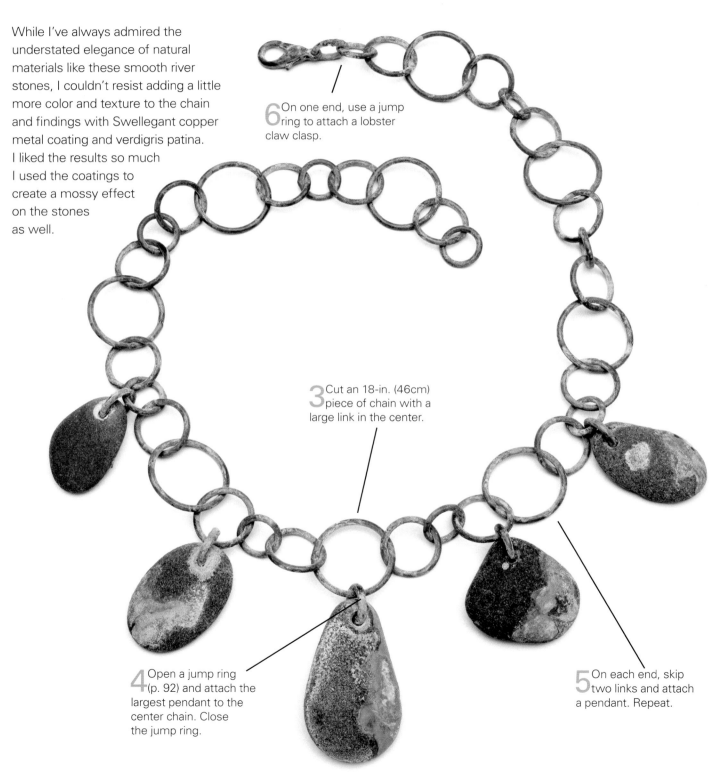

6 On one end, use a jump ring to attach a lobster claw clasp.

3 Cut an 18-in. (46cm) piece of chain with a large link in the center.

4 Open a jump ring (p. 92) and attach the largest pendant to the center chain. Close the jump ring.

5 On each end, skip two links and attach a pendant. Repeat.

NECKLACE

1 With a paintbrush, dab the brass metal coating on the (clean and dry) chain, jump rings, and clasp. Let the first layer dry for 5–10 minutes and apply a second layer.

2 Apply a third layer of metal coating. While it's still wet, liberally brush on the patina. To get a mossy effect on the pendants, brush metal coating on a section of river stone (allowing some metal to show through on the stones). Set aside to let the color develop. The time it takes for the color to bloom will vary, but allow at least an hour to get the full effect. Allow to dry for 72 hours. Apply the sealant with a brush.

EARRINGS

For each earring: Brush metal coating on a section of river stone. Refer to the necklace step 2 and add patina. Allow some metal to show through on the stones. Repeat necklace steps 1 and 2 to add color to the jump rings and the earring wires. Open a jump ring (p. 92) and string a river stone. Close the jump ring. Open the loop of an earring wire. Attach the bead unit and close the loop.

(p. 92)

5 tips for successful color coating

Use thick-gauge jump rings to match the thick chain.

The metal coating adds thickness to the jump rings. If your jump rings are a tight fit with the stones, add patina to them (carefully) after you string them through the pendants.

If you don't want to add thickness and texture to the findings, skip the metal coating and apply patina directly to the metal.

For a reversible look, keep the "moss" on one side of the pendant.

Go to cforiginals.com and download the Swellegant PDF for more tips.

Suitable for stringing

While the term "too beautiful to eat" has never stopped me, "too beautiful to string" has often been a creative stumbling block. Lampworked or other one-of-a-kind focal masterpieces have a hard time making it from my work table into a project because I am paralyzed by fear of not doing them justice.

My simple solution for Lisa Kan's "Haiku" bead lets the focal bead shine, and adds visual impact. Lisa's bead has a background of both cool and warm blues with accents of olive green and peach, all wrapped up with delicate black lines.

5 On each end over both wires, string a crimp bead, a color A rondelle, and half of a clasp.

6 Check the fit and add or remove beads as needed. Go back through the beads just strung. Tighten the wire and crimp the crimp beads (p. 92). Trim the excess wire.

4 On both sides, alternate between steps 2 and 3 until the strands are within 1 in. (2.5cm) of the finished length.

2 One one end, on one wire, string 13 11º seed beads. On the other wire, string four 11ºs, a color A 6mm rondelle, an 11º, a 4mm, and an 11º. Over both wires, string a 6mm color A.

3 On the other end, on one wire, string 13 11ºs. On the other wire, string four 11ºs, a color A 6mm rondelle, an 11º, a color B 6mm rondelle, and an 11º. Over both wires, string a color A.

NECKLACE

1 Cut two 26-in. (66cm) pieces of flexible beading wire. Over both wires, center a 4mm rondelle. Over all four ends, string an art bead and 4mm rondelle.

EARRINGS

For each earring: On an eyepin, string two color A rondelles, a color C rondelle, a B rondelle, a C, and two A's. Use roundnose pliers to create a loop at the end of the wire. Use chainnose pliers to turn the loop into a coil (p. 93). Open the loop of an earring wire (p. 92). Attach the dangle and close the loop.

!i **My strands** start with black 11° seed beads with fire-polished beads in peach, olive, and warm blue. I used matte black findings in both the necklace and the earrings to tie the two pieces together.

DESIGN ALTERNATIVE

I broke my own rule with this version and used expensive gemstones, but I used less than half of the gemstone strand and supplemented with straight strung crystals.

Art beads are (justifiably) expensive. Choose budget-friendly beads for the rest of the necklace—like seed beads and fire-polished beads. The art bead will do the heavy lifting; just choose your colors wisely and let the focal bead shine.

I strung the fire-polished colors in roughly the same proportions as they appeared in the bead. First warm blue, then olive, then peach.

Bentnose pliers or nylon-jawed pliers are also handy for making coils.

Charm to spare

I bought these charms on a trip to see the cave paintings of Lascaux France a few years ago, but (as usual) it took me a while to figure out the perfect way to use them. I ruled a bracelet out immediately because I wanted all the charms—and their tiny details—to be visible at once. I struggled with finding a "not the usual" necklace design until *Bead Style*'s senior editor, Naomi Fujimoto, created a great multi-chain display for some stunning gemstones. I added my own twists to her idea by dangling the charms and pairing them with green goldstone nuggets.

When choosing beads to go with the charms, make sure they are of a comparable weight and have the same visual feel. For instance, the nuggets are an earthy tone and have a rugged shape that reflects the primitive art depicted in the charms.

NECKLACE

1 On a headpin, string a nugget. Make the first half of a wrapped loop (p. 92). Make four nugget units.

2 Cut an 8-, 9-, 10½-, and 12-in. (20, 23, 26.7, and 30cm) piece of chain. Open a 6mm jump ring (p. 92). Attach one end of each chain and close the jump ring. Repeat on the other end.

3 Hang the jump rings on the pegs of a Chain Sta. You can also use tacks to attach the jump rings to a foam board or securely tape the rings to the edge of your work table so the chains hang over the side. Use jump rings to position the charms, and attach the loops of the nuggets. Check the drape and adjust the placement of the charms and beads as needed. Don't close the jump rings or complete the wraps until all the components are placed.

4 Cut two 3–4-in. (7.6–10cm) pieces of chain. Open a jump ring on each side of the strands and attach a chain. Check the fit and trim the chain as needed.

5 On each end, open a link (or use a jump ring) to attach half of a clasp.

EARRINGS

1 For each earring: Follow necklace step 1 to make a nugget unit. Cut a 1¾-in. (4.4cm) piece of chain. Attach the nugget unit and complete the wraps.

2 On an eyepin, string a nugget. Make a plain loop (p. 92). Cut a 2-in. (5cm) piece of chain. Open the loop and attach the chain.

3 Attach the nugget unit and close the loop. Open the loop on an earring wire and attach the dangle. Close the loop.

Lighten
up

Lucite is a brand name for acrylic, which is a form of plastic. You can find new and vintage beads, as well as beads that are "vintage style." I love the color and shape options Lucite offers, but for me it's the weight (or lack thereof) that makes it perfect for big projects such as this bracelet or a multistrand statement necklace. You get abundance without bulk. If these calla lilies were made of a heavier material, they would have eventually stretched out the coils of the memory wire, making the bracelet unwearable. I was immediately attracted to the sophisticated, muted colors of these beads. Because the bead holes go through less than half of the bead, you can easily string them on the rigidly curved coil, creating unexpected texture.

BRACELET

1 Cut five coils of memory wire (see memory wire tips on p. 79 before cutting). Make a loop on one end with roundnose pliers (p. 92).

2 String a calla lily bead (with the opening facing the loop) and a nugget spacer. Repeat until your bracelet is the desired length.

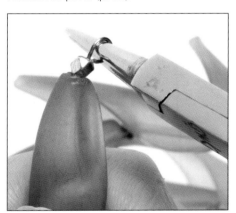

3 Trim the end of the coil to ¼ in. (6mm) and make a loop.

3 little design details

To get the color-blocked look, I used two strands of moss green, two strand of gray blue, one strand of indigo, and one strand of lavender. The pattern I used was:

moss green
gray blue
½ indigo
lavender
½ indigo
moss green

I had an extra strand of lavender to use for earrings, but I could have pulled a moss green bead from either end for the earrings also.

For the earrings, I made the wrapped loops on the dangles with extra wraps to keep them in proportion with the long beads.

EARRINGS

For each earring: On a headpin, string three nuggets, a calla lily bead (opening first), and a nugget. Make a wrapped loop (p. 92). Open the loop of an earring wire (p. 92) and attach a bead unit. Close the loop.

I'll take bicones with everything

Crystal bicones are the world's most glamorous workhorses. 4mm bicones are my go-to choice for many (if not most) of my designs. Whether they're accents or, as in this necklace and earrings, the main attraction, their ready availability and variety of colors make them the answer to a range of design questions.

I added some subtle variation to this monochromatic design by mixing satin and AB (aurora borealis) versions with the amethyst bicones. I used crystal metallic light gold 2ABs to anchor the design and link the circles.

NECKLACE

1 Cut a 50-in. (1.28m) piece of beading wire. On the wire, center: color A 4mm bicone, two color B 4mm bicones, 8mm bicone pendant, two Bs, an A, and a B.

2 Bring the wire through the last bicone strung (B) in the opposite direction. Tighten the loop.

3 On one end, bring the wire through the adjacent A. String three color C 4mms, an A, and three Cs.

4 Go back through the A and the first four bicones added in step 3. The wire should exit the A. Tighten the loop. Repeat, substituting color Ds for the Cs.

5 String four Bs, two A's, and two Bs. Go back through the A and the first five bicones added. The wire should exit the A. Repeat steps 3 and 4.

6 String two Bs, two A's, and four Bs. Go back through the A and the first three bicones added. The wire should exit the A. Repeat steps 3 and 4.

4 crystal finish tips

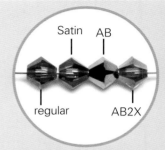

AB (aurora borealis) is an iridescent coating that adds a multicolored effect. The AB finish is normally applied to half of a bead. AB2X means the coating has been applied to the entire bead.

The satin effect is not a coating but a deeper, more saturated color in the crystal.

I didn't use the AB2X version of the amethyst bicones because the color change was too drastic for my design.

Swarovski Xilion beads are bicone shaped, but they have extra faceting for more sparkle, and a rounded hole for better thread protection.

7 On the other end, repeat steps 3–6. On each end, string 4mm bicones until the necklace is within 1 in. (2.5cm) of the finished length. I used Bs and finished with 1 in. (2.5cm) of A's.

8 On each end, string a crimp bead, a bicone, and half of a clasp. Check the fit and add or remove beads as needed. Go back through the beads just strung. Tighten the wire and crimp the crimp bead (p. 92). Trim the excess wire.

EARRINGS

1 For each earring: Insert an earring post in an eraser or sponge to keep the cup level. Prepare two-part epoxy according to package directions. Fill the cup halfway and insert the drilled end of an 8mm bicone pendant. Let dry.

2 On a headpin, string a color A 4mm bicone. Make a plain loop (p. 92). On an eyepin, string a color C 4mm and make a plain loop. Make another eyepin unit with an color D 4mm.

3 Open the plain loops and connect the bicone units as shown (color C on top). Attach the dangle to the loop of the earring post.

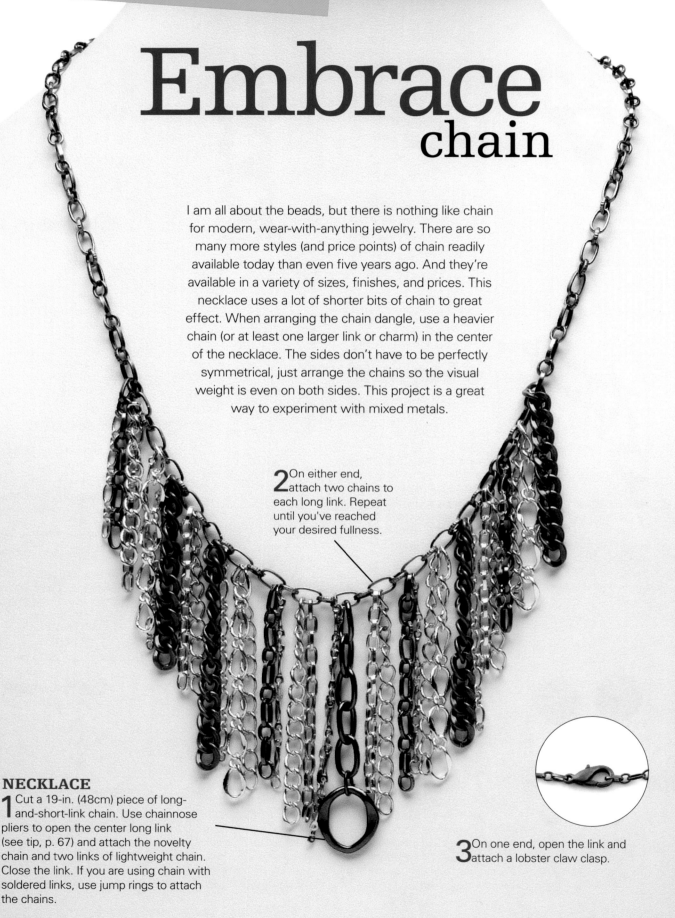

Embrace
chain

I am all about the beads, but there is nothing like chain for modern, wear-with-anything jewelry. There are so many more styles (and price points) of chain readily available today than even five years ago. And they're available in a variety of sizes, finishes, and prices. This necklace uses a lot of shorter bits of chain to great effect. When arranging the chain dangle, use a heavier chain (or at least one larger link or charm) in the center of the necklace. The sides don't have to be perfectly symmetrical, just arrange the chains so the visual weight is even on both sides. This project is a great way to experiment with mixed metals.

2 On either end, attach two chains to each long link. Repeat until you've reached your desired fullness.

NECKLACE

1 Cut a 19-in. (48cm) piece of long-and-short-link chain. Use chainnose pliers to open the center long link (see tip, p. 67) and attach the novelty chain and two links of lightweight chain. Close the link. If you are using chain with soldered links, use jump rings to attach the chains.

3 On one end, open the link and attach a lobster claw clasp.

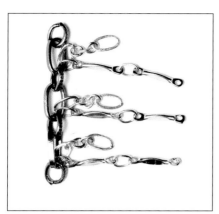

EARRINGS

For each earring: Cut a 1¼ in. (3.2cm) piece of long-and-short chain, beginning and ending with short links. Cut three ¾-in. (1.9cm) type-A chains and three ¼-in. (6mm) type-B chains. Attach a type-A chain and a type-B chain to each long link on the long-and-short chain either by opening a chain link or using a jump ring. Open the loop of an earring wire. Attach a dangle and close the loop.

To cut even pieces of chain, hang the chains on a pin and trim the ends.

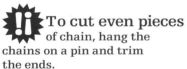

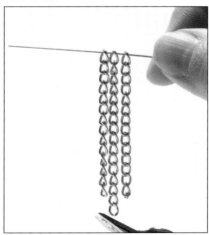

COMMON CHAIN STYLES

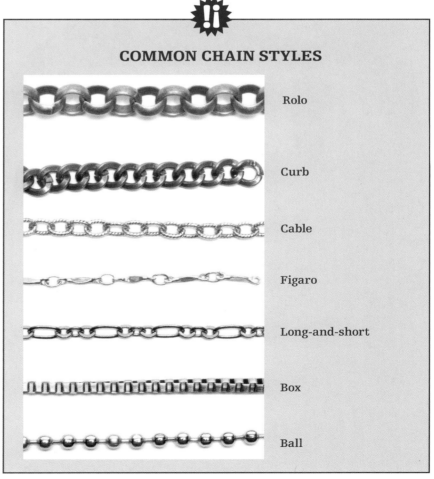

Rolo

Curb

Cable

Figaro

Long-and-short

Box

Ball

Blue-ribbon style

Jane Konkel, associate editor at *Bead Style*, is a big fan of ribbon bracelets. I think it's because it's almost impossible to put one on yourself, and Jane's a big fan of connecting with people. I couldn't agree more. I also like the bright washes of soft color and the snuggly way they feel on your wrist. I added a little silvery glow to this one by spacing some pewter components from Green Girl Studios along the fabric, but for a quick grown-up friendship bracelet, just center a striking button and leave it at that. Give your friend a second bracelet to share with someone else. I have yet to find a design for ribbon earrings that I really liked, so I made a pair that goes with anything—including the bracelet.

BRACELET

1 On the ribbon, center a button.

2 Position the button on the front of your wrist. Wrap the ribbon back and forth around your arm, tying the ends in front.

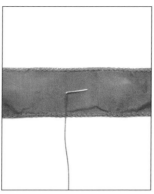

3 Use paper clips to mark the desired position of two charms—one on each side of your arm.

4 Unwrap the ribbon, keeping the clips in place. Cut a 6-in. (15cm) piece of wire. Make a 90-degree bend at the end of the wire.

5 Remove a marker, and wrap the wire a few times around the ribbon, crossing the bent piece of wire. Wrap around an open jump ring, then continue wrapping the wire several times around the ribbon.

6 a. Tuck the wire through two or three wraps and trim the excess wire. Attach a charm and close the jump ring.
b. Repeat steps 4–6a with the second charm.

7 Attach a third charm at one end of the ribbon.

3 tips for customized details

Depending on the type of charms you use, you can attach them with a jump ring or attach them directly. I used one of each on this bracelet. The bird charm at the end of the ribbon started as a large-hole bead. I made the charm by stringing a 4mm bead and the bird bead on a headpin and making a wrapped loop. I strung the wrapped loop on the ribbon, then secured it with wraps on each side.

Your wraps can be neat or freeform as long as they are tight enough to stay secure. Make sure the ends are tucked in so they don't tear the ribbon or poke your skin.

Never open a jump ring by pulling the ends away from each other. Open and close a jump ring (or loop) with a back and forth (scissors) motion (see p. 92).

EARRINGS

1 On an eyepin, string a lentil bead. Make a plain loop (p. 92). Make a second lentil unit.

2 For the first earring, open a loop (p. 92) and attach the key charm. Close the loop.

3 For the second earring, cut a ½-in. (1.3cm) piece of chain.

4 Attach one end of the chain to the lentil bead unit. Open a jump ring and attach the lock charm to the end of the chain. Close the jump ring.

5 For each earring: Open the loop of an earring wire. Attach the dangle and close the loop.

Fashion favors the bold

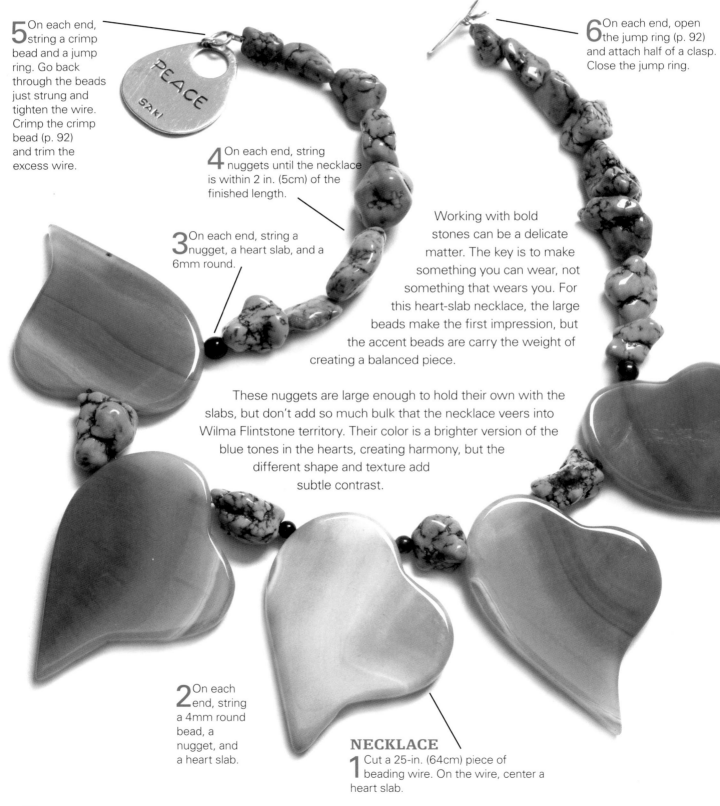

5 On each end, string a crimp bead and a jump ring. Go back through the beads just strung and tighten the wire. Crimp the crimp bead (p. 92) and trim the excess wire.

6 On each end, open the jump ring (p. 92) and attach half of a clasp. Close the jump ring.

4 On each end, string nuggets until the necklace is within 2 in. (5cm) of the finished length.

3 On each end, string a nugget, a heart slab, and a 6mm round.

Working with bold stones can be a delicate matter. The key is to make something you can wear, not something that wears you. For this heart-slab necklace, the large beads make the first impression, but the accent beads are carry the weight of creating a balanced piece.

These nuggets are large enough to hold their own with the slabs, but don't add so much bulk that the necklace veers into Wilma Flintstone territory. Their color is a brighter version of the blue tones in the hearts, creating harmony, but the different shape and texture add subtle contrast.

2 On each end, string a 4mm round bead, a nugget, and a heart slab.

NECKLACE
1 Cut a 25-in. (64cm) piece of beading wire. On the wire, center a heart slab.

DESIGN ALTERNATIVE

Sometimes one bold stone is enough. The round beads are an effective transition to the chain. String all three beads on a 4-in. (10cm) piece of 20-gauge wire and make a wrapped loop (p. 92) on each end, connecting the chain before you complete the wraps.

3 weighty tips

With large beads, use a large clasp for visual balance.

Choose the best flexible beading wire:

- .010: seed beads, freshwater pearls, and smaller gemstones

- .012–.013: crystals, seed beads, pearls

- .014–.019: medium to heavy beads and gemstones, crystals, seed beads, glass and metal beads.

These are the sizes most commonly used:

- .020/.021: large, heavy gemstones with unevenly drilled holes for medium-weight designs

- .024/.026: large, heavy beads with large holes

- .030/.036: large, chunky, heavy beads, and large crystals

When you make a bold necklace, keep the earrings small.

EARRINGS

For each earring: On a headpin, string a 6mm round bead and a nugget. Make a wrapped loop (p. 92). Open the loop of an earring wire (p. 92). Attach the dangle and close the loop.

Playing it cool: mix silver textures and tones

With so many different silver and silver-toned beads available, mixing and matching couldn't be easier. There are designers who won't use anything but fine and sterling silver, but my creative side (backed up by my budget) tells me to mix things up. Don't deny yourself the beauty of Thai silver beads just because you can't afford a whole necklace. Surround them with a multi-textured collection of humbler supporting players, plus the subtle visual snap of a few blue beads. I added even more dimension by cutting apart chain links and stringing them around the coin-shaped beads. I kept the earrings simple by using the smallest beads in the necklace with distinctive earring wires.

5 Check the fit and add or remove beads as needed. Go back through the beads strung. Tighten the wire and crimp the crimp beads. Trim the excess wire. On each end, open the figure-8 connector and attach half of a clasp. Close the connector.

3 On each end, string a symmetrical pattern of silver beads and links.

NECKLACE

1 Cut a 31-in. (79cm) piece of beading wire. Center two large beads.

2 On one end, string a Hill Tribes silver bead. On the other end, string a blue bead, a Hill Tribes silver bead, and a blue bead.

EARRINGS

For each earring: On a headpin, string a bead and make a wrapped loop. Open the loop of an earring wire and attach the bead unit. Close the loop.

4 On each end, string a crimp bead and a figure-8 connector.

7 !! things to know about silver

Fine silver is 99% silver. Sterling silver is a mixture of 92.5% silver and another metal, usually copper.

Sterling silver will tarnish in time and needs to be cleaned unless you like an antiqued look.

For a natural way to remove tarnish from sterling silver, pour hot water into a foil-lined pan. Add a cup of baking soda and some salt, and stir until dissolved. Put silver beads or jewelry into the water one at a time to remove tarnish.

Store sterling silver beads and jewelry in plastic bags with a piece of chalk to slow the tarnishing process.

German silver is a mixture of copper, zinc, and nickel and actually contains no silver.

Bali, East Indian, Israeli, or Mexican silver is sterling; Hill Tribes (Thai) silver is 95–98% pure.

See p. 67 for an explanation of the terms plate, filled, and finished.

!! The chain used for the links had figure-8 connectors. I used two to give the finishing a little more flexibility.

!! When a cool blue bead (like navy) is mixed with silver, the effect is harmonious. Using a warm blue (turquoise or aqua) creates more contrast and makes each element pop. Using even warmer colors like red or orange or yellowish green with silver creates even more contrast (right).

Gold standard

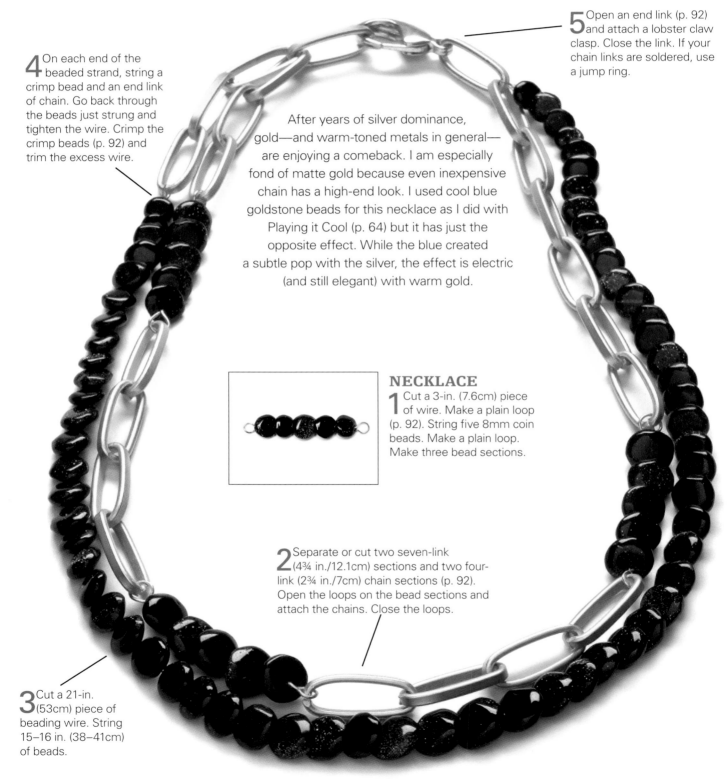

5 Open an end link (p. 92) and attach a lobster claw clasp. Close the link. If your chain links are soldered, use a jump ring.

4 On each end of the beaded strand, string a crimp bead and an end link of chain. Go back through the beads just strung and tighten the wire. Crimp the crimp beads (p. 92) and trim the excess wire.

After years of silver dominance, gold—and warm-toned metals in general—are enjoying a comeback. I am especially fond of matte gold because even inexpensive chain has a high-end look. I used cool blue goldstone beads for this necklace as I did with Playing it Cool (p. 64) but it has just the opposite effect. While the blue created a subtle pop with the silver, the effect is electric (and still elegant) with warm gold.

NECKLACE

1 Cut a 3-in. (7.6cm) piece of wire. Make a plain loop (p. 92). String five 8mm coin beads. Make a plain loop. Make three bead sections.

2 Separate or cut two seven-link (4¾ in./12.1cm) sections and two four-link (2¾ in./7cm) chain sections (p. 92). Open the loops on the bead sections and attach the chains. Close the loops.

3 Cut a 21-in. (53cm) piece of beading wire. String 15–16 in. (38–41cm) of beads.

When opening the chain links, make sure you grip the links with as much surface area of the pliers as possible.

!! **Diagonally drilled** coin-shaped beads are pretty unusual. If you find some, be sure to gently flatten the head of the headpin against the bead when making a bead unit. If you use regular coin pearls, you'll need fewer beads for the beaded sections of the necklace.

EARRINGS

For each earring: Cut or separate one chain link. On a headpin, string a 8mm coin bead. Make the first half of a wrapped loop. Make three dangles. Attach each dangle to the link and complete the wraps. Open the loop of an earring wire. Attach the dangle and close the loop.

4 !! golden facts

A karat refers to the amount of actual pure gold in the gold. 14K indicates 14 parts gold out of 24, or 58% pure. 24K is 100% pure gold. The remaining parts are usually silver, copper, or other metal. The metal the gold is mixed with affects the color—green, rose, yellow, or white. Most commercial gold is 14–24K.

Gold plated refers to a very thin layer of gold electroplated or electrochemically applied to another metal. Gold-filled refers to a layer of gold applied with heat or pressure. It is usually thicker than plating.

Vermeil is a sterling silver base heavily electroplated with 22K gold.

Gold-finished refers to a base metal electroplated with a nonstandard (usually very thin) layer of gold.

ALTERNATIVE

Light topaz crystals are almost the same tone as the gold charm chain in this bracelet and earrings. They add a new texture and a different way to catch the light, rather than a new color.

Mining for the right
copper mix

Copper is a metal, but in this necklace, the ember-hot color is represented by gemstones, lampworked glass, and seed beads. Even the metal itself is variously represented—by the natural bright as well as the antiqued versions. The unifying warm tones make it all work together beautifully.

4 On each end, string a spacer, a lampworked bead, a spacer, and a 3¾-in. (9.5cm) alternating pattern of briolettes and 11ºs.

2 Cut 25-in. (64cm) piece of beading wire. On the beading wire, center the end link of the 6-in. (15cm) chain, 4mm daisy spacer, 12mm lampworked bead, spacer, 23mm carved bead, spacer, lampworked bead, spacer, carved bead, spacer, lampworked bead, spacer, end link of chain.

NECKLACE

1 Separate or cut a 6-in. (15cm) piece of chain and two 3-in. (7.6cm) pieces of chain.

3 On each end, string an end link of a 3-in. (7.6cm) chain, a 2¼-in. (5.7cm) alternating pattern of 5x7mm briolettes and 11º seed beads, and an end link of the chain.

!! **If you want to be able** to adjust the drape of your chain segments, cut larger pieces and experiment with stringing different links before cutting the chain to the proper length.

5 On each end, string four 11°s, a crimp bead, and half of a clasp. Check the fit and add or remove 11°s as needed.

6 Go back through the beads just strung and tighten the wire. Crimp the crimp beads and trim the excess wire.

!! **I've had mixed results** with copper (as well as brass and gunmetal) crimps. Some are not very sturdy and practically crumble when crimped. Make sure you have a reputable brand of crimps or use gold-filled crimps.

EARRINGS

For each earring: Cut a 2-in. (5cm) piece of beading wire. String six 11° seed beads, a 5x7mm briolette, an 11°, a briolette, and six 11°s. String both ends through a crimp bead and two adjacent beads in opposite directions. Tighten the wire and make a flattened crimp (p. 92). Trim the excess wire. Separate a four-link section of chain. Open an end link and attach the dangle. Close the link. Open the loop of an earring wire. Attach the dangle and close the loop.

!! # 6 tips to cover the bases

Copper is a base metal—the term refers to any metal that isn't precious (gold, silver, platinum, rhodium).

Many findings are copper plated rather than pure copper for strength's sake.

Copper is a soft metal that isn't very durable unless it is mixed with another stronger metal.

Brass is a base metal composed of 70% copper and 30% zinc; gunmetal is dark colored "red" brass.

Nickel silver is an alloy of mostly nickel that resembles sterling silver.

Pewter is an alloy of tin and small amounts of antimony and copper. Genuine pewter contains lead, but lead-free pewter is available for jewelry making.

Clear
and present style

Using clear beads doesn't always mean abandoning color—it's a great way to give brightly patterned chain the spotlight. But even if you use traditional silver chain, lack of color does not mean lack of interest or style. Jewelry using only clear beads is a goes-with-every-thing staple for any wardrobe and a foolproof gift. Add some extra interest by playing with shapes and textures among the beads.

SILVER-CHAIN NECKLACE

1 On a headpin, string a clear bead. Make the first half of a wrapped loop (p. 92). Make seven rough-cut crystal units, six round bead units, and eight oval beads units. Cut a 21-in. (53cm) piece of 4mm-link chain. Center a rough-cut crystal unit and complete the wraps.

2 On each side, skipping one link between each bead unit, attach a round bead unit, an oval bead unit, and a crystal bead unit, completing the wraps as you go. Repeat twice.

3 Open the jump ring (p. 92). On one end of the chain, attach a lobster claw clasp and close the jump ring. Repeat on the other end, omitting the clasp.

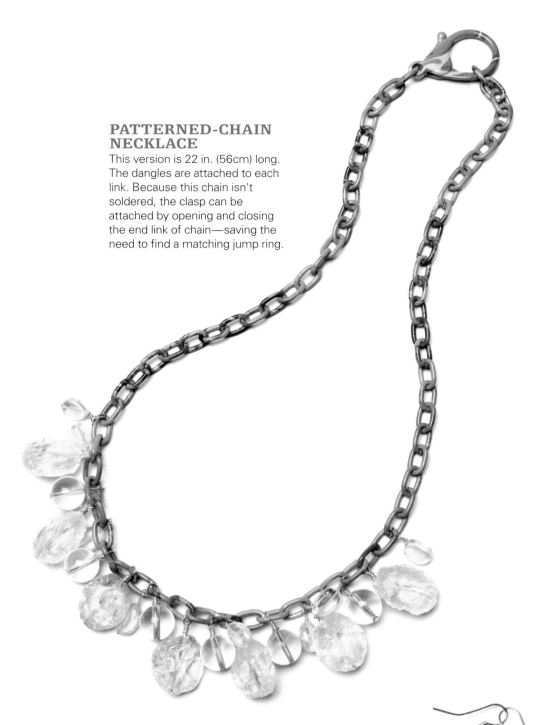

PATTERNED-CHAIN NECKLACE

This version is 22 in. (56cm) long. The dangles are attached to each link. Because this chain isn't soldered, the clasp can be attached by opening and closing the end link of chain—saving the need to find a matching jump ring.

3 tips for seeing clearly

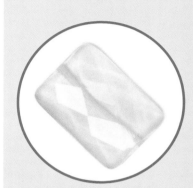

Opalescent beads add just a hint of color but don't clash with nearby hues.

Partially brushed crystals add a hint of texture to an otherwise clear color palette.

Consider using colored craft wire or findings to take full advantage of transparent beads.

PATTERNED-CHAIN EARRINGS

For each earring: Following silver chain necklace step 1, make a rough-cut crystal unit. Separate a two-link piece of chain. Attach a bead unit and complete the wraps. Open the loop of an earring wire (p. 92). Attach the dangle and close the loop.

Take a (short) walk on the wild side

I've always admired women who can carry off bold statement necklaces with exotic beads. I've never quite been able to pull off that look. I realize that perception is mostly in my head, but it seems easier to modify a jewelry design than to reboot my personality. Using a few carved wood beads with classic pearls or adding a few pearls to African recycled glass beads gives me just the right amount of visual excitement. You can adjust the ratio to match your own taste for adventure.

5 On each end, go back through the beads just strung and tighten the wire. Crimp the crimp bead (p. 92) and trim the excess wire.

4 On each end, string a 9mm pearl, a crimp bead, and half of a clasp.

3 On each end, string an alternating pattern with 10 flat spacers and nine 11mm pearls.

2 On each end, string an alternating pattern with three flat spacers and three 13mm pearls.

CARVED WOOD NECKLACE

1 Cut a 24-in. (61cm) piece of beading wire. Center an alternating pattern with three wood beads and two flat spacers.

CARVED WOOD EARRINGS

For each earring: On a decorative headpin, string a 9mm pearl, a flat spacer, and a carved wood bead. Make a wrapped loop (p. 92). Open the loop of an earring wire (p. 92). Attach the dangle and close the loop.

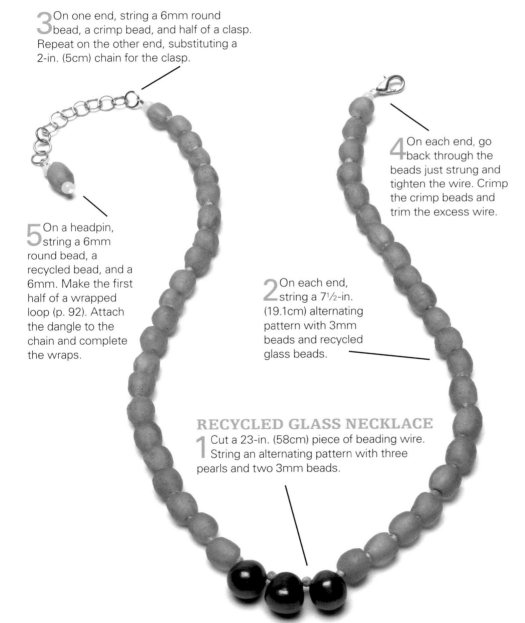

3 On one end, string a 6mm round bead, a crimp bead, and half of a clasp. Repeat on the other end, substituting a 2-in. (5cm) chain for the clasp.

5 On a headpin, string a 6mm round bead, a recycled bead, and a 6mm. Make the first half of a wrapped loop (p. 92). Attach the dangle to the chain and complete the wraps.

4 On each end, go back through the beads just strung and tighten the wire. Crimp the crimp beads and trim the excess wire.

2 On each end, string a 7½-in. (19.1cm) alternating pattern with 3mm beads and recycled glass beads.

RECYCLED GLASS NECKLACE

1 Cut a 23-in. (58cm) piece of beading wire. String an alternating pattern with three pearls and two 3mm beads.

---

4 **!!**
beading wire tips

Flexible beading wire is composed of wires twisted together and coated with nylon.

It's stronger than beading thread and won't stretch (although it will kink). The higher the strand count, the more flexible and kink-resistant the wire. In general, use the thickest wire that will go through your beads.

When reading beading wire labels, remember the decimal refers to the wire diameter in inches (i.e., .014 beading wire has a diameter of .014 inches).

When choosing flexible beading wire, use:

- .010 or .012 to string lightweight beads or beads with small holes, such as seed beads or pearls.

- .014 or .015 for most gemstones, crystals, and glass beads. If you buy only one spool of wire, start with .014 or .015.

- .018 or .019 for mediumweight beads.

- .024 or .036 for heavy beads and nuggets.

Find your balance

4 On each end, string a crimp bead and half of a clasp. Check the fit and add or remove beads as needed.

5 Go back through the beads just strung. Tighten the wires and crimp the crimp beads (p. 92). Trim the excess wire.

I love the look of asymmetrical designs. Their sense of balance is dynamic and informal and—to me—more fun. Despite its informal feel, asymmetry actually takes deliberate planning to achieve. If you have a very large off-center bead as in the fish necklace, make sure the rest of the strand is strung with heavy enough beads to keep the large bead in position when the necklace is worn. The feel of balance can also be created visually, with color, or with bead size, as in the druzy necklace.

2 On one end, string 6 in. (15cm) of nuggets and rondelles.

3 On the other end, string 11 in. (28cm) of nuggets and rondelles.

FISH NECKLACE

1 Cut a 26-in. (66cm) piece of beading wire (p. 92). On the wire, string apatite and aquamarine rondelles, a fish bead, and apatite and aquamarine rondelles.

FISH EARRINGS For each earring: On a headpin, string a fish bead and a pinch bead. Make a plain loop (p. 92). On a headpin, string a nugget and make a plain loop. Cut a 2½-in. (6.4cm) piece of chain. Open the loop on the fish bead unit (p. 92) and attach it to the end link of the chain. Close the loop. Attach the nugget unit to the other end of the chain. Open the loop of an earring wire. Attach the dangle so the fish hangs lower than the nugget. Close the loop. Hang the nugget lower on the second earring.

5 Go back through the beads just strung. Tighten the wires and crimp the crimp beads (p. 92). Trim the excess wire.

4 On each end, string a crimp bead and half of a clasp. Check the fit and add or remove beads as needed.

2 On one end, string 4 in. (10cm) of 8mm top-drilled nuggets.

3 On the other end, string 2 in. (5cm) of top-drilled nuggets, two 22mm, a rondelles, two 22mms, and 3½ in. (8.9cm) of top-drilled nuggets.

!i **To change the** position of the focal bead, remove beads from the side you want to move the focal closer to and add them to the other side.

!i **If you want to** change the length of the necklace, but not the position of the focal, add or remove beads equally from both sides.

DRUZY NECKLACE

1 Cut a 24-in. (61cm) piece of beading wire (p. 92). On the wire string two 22mm nuggets, a druzy bead, and a 22mm.

CREATIVITY BOOST!

You've just explored the possibilities of a treasure trove of different materials, but there are so many more design options just waiting for you. The next projects will help you push your creative boundaries.

The *Refresh Your Memory Wire* bracelet starts with the simplest of materials and adds some basic wire wraps and colorful beads to create a trendy bangle. I used round beads, but this bracelet will work with ovals or nuggets or whatever combination your imagination can conceive.

Act Two frees that old, not-quite-there necklace—the one with more nostalgia than style—from the dusty bottom of your dresser drawer. Spice it up with some fresh beads and a new idea or two, and you've turned forgotten into fabulous.

Every jewelry box should have at least one pearl necklace, but your pearls don't have to look like everybody else's. Be classic without ever being predictable by looking at pearls a whole new way. Change the shape or turn up the color volume—or both. *New Pearl in Town* will get you started.

All of these projects were designed to be sparks for your own inspiration. Your ideas, sense of style, and materials you may already have in your stash can turn one idea into a dozen.

Refresh your
memory wire

Memory wire is easy to dismiss for a beader who enjoys a challenge. It's almost too easy. Other than deciding on how you will finish the ends, it's pretty much just stringing on the beads. And if you're looking for a quick spiral cuff, what's wrong with that?

If you're like me, you're always looking to create something new. I love to push my skills and find a new use for an old favorite. This wire-wrapped cuff was inspired by the designer Chan Luu's leather wrap bracelets. My cuff is more structural then Chan Luu's, but the wrapping technique is virtually identical.

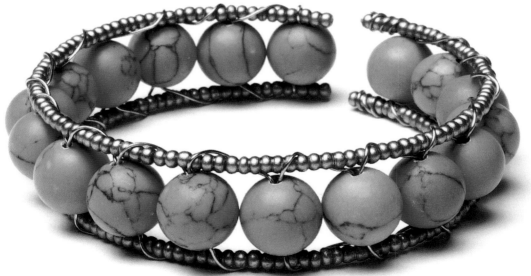

Memory wire cuffs make great gifts because they're one-size-fits-all. If you sell your jewelry they're a quick way to add items with lower price points to your inventory.

Gluing can be a bit of a mess, so you may be tempted to take a short-cut and glue only the seed beads on each end of the coil. For the sake of security, glue every bead to the wire. Wrapping the wire will require a good deal of tugging and tightening. Two-part epoxy is strong, but it's unwise to expect a few seed beads to carry the burden of the whole coil.

If you're not in a hurry, I'd recommend gluing half of each coil and then letting dry before gluing the other half. Otherwise, at some point you'll have to hold a not-quite-dry portion of the coil to string the last few beads.

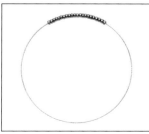

BRACELET

1 Cut one complete memory wire coil. Mix two-part epoxy according to package directions. Working in 1-in. (2.5cm) segments, apply epoxy to the wire, then string seed beads over the glued area until the entire coil in covered in seed beads. Make a second coil. Allow to dry.

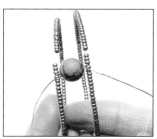

2 Cut a 24-in. (61cm) piece of 24-gauge wire. Center a 10mm bead on the wire. Position the bead between the memory wire coils. Bring the wire over and around the coils and back through the bead in the opposite direction. Tighten the wire.

! **You can use 26-gauge** or even 28-gauge wire to wrap—and you might have to with gemstones with small holes—but you'll need to take greater care when wrapping and tightening the wire.

3 Bring each end of the wire over and around the memory wire coils. Bring the ends through a 10mm bead in opposite directions. Tighten the wire. Repeat until you reach the end of the coils.

4 Wrap the wire around the coils twice and trim the excess wire.

EARRINGS

For each earring: Cut one complete memory wire coil. Mix two-part epoxy according to package directions. Apply the epoxy to a 1½-in. (3.8cm) segment at the end of the coil. String a seed bead, a 10mm bead, and a seed bead. Allow to dry. Use a metal file or emery board to file the sharp point at the other end of the coil.

2 memory wire tips **!**

Never, EVER use regular jewelry wire cutters on memory wire. If you do, you might as well toss them into your garbage can. Heavy-duty wire cutters are relatively inexpensive and can be found at the hardware store.

In a pinch, you can grip the point where you want to sever the wire with chainnose pliers and bend the memory wire back and forth until it snaps.

6 finishing options **!**

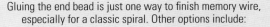

Gluing the end bead is just one way to finish memory wire, especially for a classic spiral. Other options include:

- Folding over the ends instead of making a loop
- Creating a loop on each end (with this option, a bead dangle is a nice touch)
- Gluing a half-drilled bead
- Using a Scrimp or a Scrimp cable end. Scrimps are screw-on (and off) crimp beads
- Adding a security chain if you are using heavier beads on a memory coil

Act two

I think all of us has a
few old necklaces in our jewelry boxes.
There is something that keeps us from tossing
them, but there's also something that keeps us from
wearing them. Give them new life by taking the components
you like and adding (or subtracting) until you have something that
fits your style.

My mom's old mother-of-pearl necklace always seemed too subdued, but I
loved the soft shimmer of the leaves. Each was drilled with two holes, which
makes them a challenge to string, but I killed two birds with one stone by making
them into dangles with colorful bicone crystals and wire. I chose a bright Mardi
Gras palette that reminded me of the colorful palettes *Bead Style*'s assistant
editor Kelsey Lawler gravitates toward. But a palette of soft blues (my usual
choice) would have added needed (though subtler) life to a lackluster necklace.
Your abandoned jewelry will come with its own challenges. The key is having
a style goal in mind and knowing what you need to get there.

I realize the chances of you having a graduated strand of double-
drilled leaves is pretty slim, but here are the steps I took to
transform my necklace.

NECKLACE

1 For each dangle: Cut a 2½-in. (6.4cm) piece of 22-gauge wire. String 1–3 4mm bicones on the wire. Bring both ends through the charm. Twist one end around the other, and trim the shorter wire.

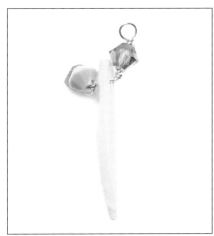

2 Bend the wire at a right angle. String a bicone and make a wrapped loop. Cut a 22-in. (56cm) piece of beading wire. On the wire, center the largest dangle. On each end, string a bicone.

3 String an alternating pattern of charms and bicones. Instead of stringing all the leaves in descending order, I mixed in some small dangles among the largest center ones. On each end, continue stringing bicones until the strand is within 1 in. (2.5cm) of the finished length. On each end, string a crimp bead, a bicone, and half of a clasp.

Check the fit and add or remove beads as needed. Go back through the beads just strung. Tighten the wire. Crimp the crimp bead (p. 92) and trim the excess wire.

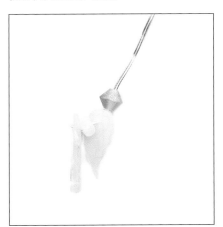

EARRINGS

1 For each earring: Cut a 2½-in. (6.4cm) piece of wire. Bring both ends through a leaf. String a seed bead on each end. On both ends, string a leaf.

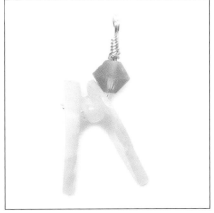

2 Over both ends, string a bicone. Make a wrapped loop (p. 92).

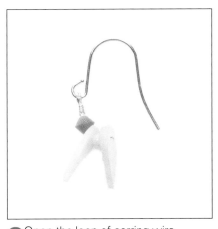

3 Open the loop of earring wire. Attach the dangle and close the loop.

This is what my necklace looked like before reconstruction. The simple graduated placement of the beads was too plain for my tastes.

 Color notes: For the dangles, I used bicones in turquoise, fire opal matte AB, tanzanite, indicolite, and erinite. For the strand, I used fire opal with tanzanite.

Classic necklace lengths
Choker or collar: 13–16 in. (33–41cm)
Princess: 17–19 in. (43–48cm)
Matinee: 20–24 in. (51–61cm)
Opera: 28–32 in. (71–81cm)
Rope and lariat: 40 in. or longer (1m+)

New pearl in town

A classic is classic for a reason—it stands the test of time. A strand of round pearls is never going to go out of style, but that doesn't mean we can't give it a new twist now and then. This multicolored design goes a step beyond classic cream and then takes another fashion leap by adding strands of fine chain for some extra swing.

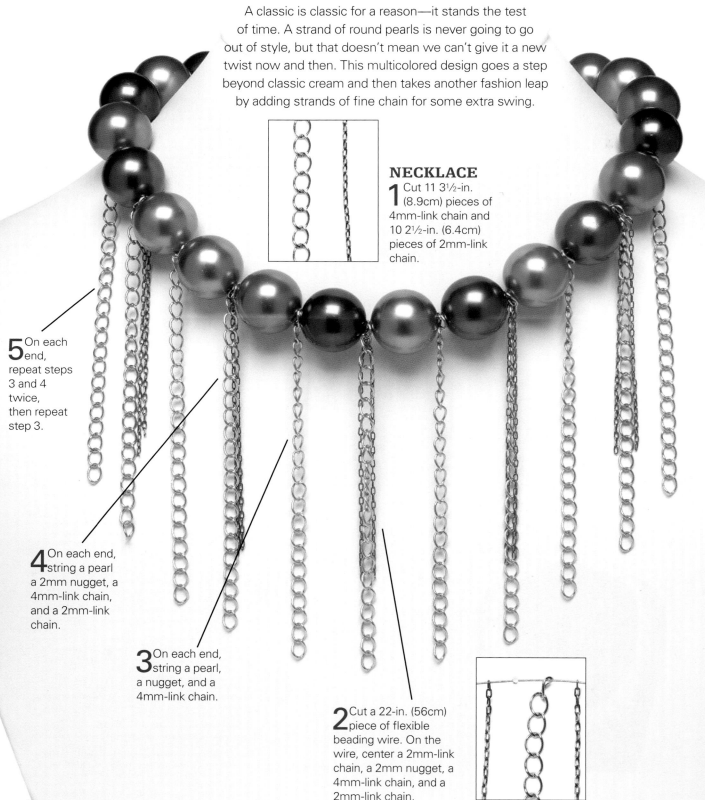

NECKLACE

1 Cut 11 3½-in. (8.9cm) pieces of 4mm-link chain and 10 2½-in. (6.4cm) pieces of 2mm-link chain.

5 On each end, repeat steps 3 and 4 twice, then repeat step 3.

4 On each end, string a pearl a 2mm nugget, a 4mm-link chain, and a 2mm-link chain.

3 On each end, string a pearl, a nugget, and a 4mm-link chain.

2 Cut a 22-in. (56cm) piece of flexible beading wire. On the wire, center a 2mm-link chain, a 2mm nugget, a 4mm-link chain, and a 2mm-link chain.

6 On each end, continue stringing pearls and nuggets until the strand is within 1 in. (2.5cm) of the finished length.

7 On each end, string a twisted crimp and half of a clasp.

8 Check the fit and add or remove pearls and nuggets as needed. Go back through the beads just strung. Tighten the wire and flatten the crimp beads. Trim the excess wire.

EARRINGS

For each earring: Cut a 2½-in. (6.4cm) piece of chain. On a headpin, string a 2mm spacer, a 4mm spacer, the 6th link of the chain, a pearl, and the end link of the chain. Make a wrapped loop (p. 92). Open the loop of an earring wire (p. 92). Attach the dangle and close the loop.

ALTERNATIVE
Try smooth nugget glass pearls with just the fine chain.

8 !i common pearl types

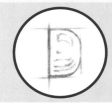
Button pearls are rounded on one side and flat on the other. They can be drilled lengthwise, through the center, or double drilled.

Coin pearls are flat and disk shaped. They also come in shapes including teardrops, triangles, and squares. They can be edge drilled or from front to back.

Faceted pearls are cut after they have been harvested.

Stick pearls, or biwa pearls, are long, flat, and freeform in shape. They can be side, center, diagonally, or top drilled.

Keshi pearls form when debris enters a mollusk. The mollusk covers the debris with nacre, creating small free-form pearls that resemble cornflakes.

Potato pearls are oval or egg-shaped. They can be drilled lengthwise or diagonally.

Rice pearls are small and shaped like grains of rice. They are usually drilled lengthwise.

Imitation (faux) pearls are synthetic and therefore consistent in size, shape, and color. These pearls are manufactured from glass, plastic, clay, or other materials.

MATERIALS, SUPPLIES & TECHNIQUES

You've learned about the tools, mastered the skills, explored the materials, and pushed the creative boundaries. Yay! But even a beading insider like you needs some backup. This section gives you the last bits of information you need to really enjoy your jewelry making.

All the supply lists are gathered here to make the trip to your local bead store or online retailed a breeze. I've included a page of my favorite places to shop if you're looking for some new ideas.

I've also summarized the step-by-step basic skills that are sprinkled throughout the projects in one convenient place in case you need a quick refresher.

Finally, there's an index of all the projects, materials, and skills so your can refer back to your favorite in a flash.

Wrapped Attention p. 16

necklace 20 in. (51cm)
- 16-in. (41cm) strand 20mm keshi pearls, center-drilled
- **30–34** 16mm button pearls
- 22 in. (56cm) round chain, 8–9mm links
- flexible beading wire, .014 or .015
- **2** crimp beads
- **7**mm jump ring
- **27–32** 2-in. (5cm) decorative headpins
- lobster claw clasp
- chainnose and roundnose pliers
- diagonal wire cutters

earrings
- **2** 20mm keshi pearls
- **6** 16mm button pearls
- **2** 3-link pieces of round chain, 8–9mm links
- **6** 2-in. (2.5cm) decorative headpins
- pair of earring wires
- chainnose and roundnose pliers
- diagonal wire cutters

Bead On a Wire p. 18

bracelet
- **2** 4mm round beads
- 2 grams assorted seed beads, 6°–11°
- 30 gauge craft wire on spool
- **2** 18mm cones
- toggle clasp
- chainnose and roundnose pliers
- diagonal wire cutters
- crochet hook

earrings
- **2** 6° seed beads
- **2** 20mm twisted bar links
- **2** 7mm jump rings
- pair of earring wires
- **2** pairs of chainnose pliers or chainnose and roundnose pliers

Gild to Suit p. 20

necklace 20 in. (51cm)
- **3** 35mm flower filigrees
- **4** 24mm flower filigrees
- **22** 4mm beads, **13** round and **9** oval
- 18 in. (46cm) long-and-short-link chain, 6 and 3mm links
- **7** 8mm jump rings
- **2** 4mm jump rings (optional)
- **22** headpins
- toggle clasp
- chainnose and roundnose pliers
- diagonal wire cutters
- hole-punch pliers
- Gilders paste, Celtic bronze and African bronze
- soft cloth

earrings
- **4** 4mm beads, **2** round and **2** oval
- **2** 24mm flower filigrees
- **2** 8mm jump rings
- **4** headpins
- pair of earring wires
- chainnose and roundnose pliers
- diagonal wire cutters
- Gilder's Paste, Celtic bronze and African bronze
- soft cloth

Weave a Simple Sparkler p. 22

bracelet
- **50–70** 3mm bicones, color A
- **50–70** 3mm bicones, color B
- **50–70** 3mm bicones, color C
- 6° seed bead
- 2 grams 13° charlottes
- beading thread
- three-loop clasp with extender chain
- #12 beading needle
- scissors
- thread conditioner (optional)

earrings
- **8** 3mm bicones, color A
- **8** 3mm bicones, color B
- **8** 3mm bicones, color C
- **14** 11° seed beads or charlottes
- beading thread
- pair of earring wires
- **2** teardrop components
- #12 beading needle
- scissors
- thread conditioner (optional)

Plainly Perfect p. 24

bracelet
- **2–3** 15mm Venetian lentil beads
- **2–3** 15mm Venetian triangle beads
- **4–5** 10mm round gold beads
- 22–26 in. (56–66cm) 22-gauge half-hard wire
- round box clasp
- chainnose and roundnose pliers
- diagonal wire cutters
- **8–10** daisy spacers (optional)

earrings
- **2** 15mm Venetian lentil beads
- **2** 20mm round links
- **2** 1½-in. (3.8cm) headpins
- pair of earring wires
- chainnose and roundnose pliers
- diagonal wire cutters

Styling Your Crimps p. 26

bracelet
- **18–22** 13mm faceted rectangular beads
- **20–24** 10mm smooth nuggets
- **6** 6mm saucer beads
- **3** 5mm oval spacers
- flexible beading wire, .014 and .015
- **6** twisted crimps
- **6** crimp covers
- **6** wire guards
- three-strand box clasp
- chainnose or crimping pliers
- diagonal wire cutters

earrings
- **3** 13mm faceted rectangular beads
- **3** 10mm smooth nuggets
- **2** 3-in. (7.6cm) headpins
- pair of earring wires
- chainnose and roundnose pliers
- diagonal wire cutters

Lush Layers p. 28

necklace 18–20 in. (46–51cm)
- **3** 16-in. (41cm) strands of 20–23mm nuggets
- 8-in. (20cm) strand of 10–12mm nuggets
- **45–50** 4mm bicones
- flexible beading wire, .014 or .015
- 6 in. (15cm) 22-gauge wire, half-hard
- **6** crimp beads
- **2** 40mm cones
- toggle clasp
- chainnose and roundnose pliers
- diagonal wire cutters

earrings
- **2** 12mm gemstone nuggets
- **10** 4mm bicones
- **8** 2-in. (5cm) headpins
- pair of marquise earring wires
- chainnose and roundnose pliers
- diagonal wire cutters

Hug a Briolette Today p. 30

necklace 15 in. (38cm)
- **3** 18mm briolettes
- 6–8mm rondelle
- 25 in. (64cm) chain, 5mm links
- 24 in. (61cm) 24-gauge wire, half-hard
- **4** 7mm jump rings
- 2-in. (5cm) headpin
- lobster claw clasp
- chainnose pliers and roundnose pliers
- diagonal wire cutters

earrings
- **2** 18mm briolettes
- 2¼ in. (5.7cm) chain, 5mm links
- 16 in. (41cm) 24-gauge wire, half-hard
- pair of earring wires
- chainnose pliers and roundnose pliers
- diagonal wire cutters

Dyeing to Be Stylish p. 32

necklace 16–20 in. (41–51cm)
- **5–10** 8mm pearls
- **54–60** 6mm pearls
- **450–500** 4mm pearls
- flexible beading wire, .010 or .012
- **10** crimp beads
- 5-loop clasp
- chainnose or crimping pliers
- diagonal wire cutters
- Rit powdered dye, royal blue and mauve
- hot pot
- vinegar
- **2** 16 oz. containers
- square of tulle or a mesh bag
- paper towels

earrings
- **2** 6mm blue pearls
- **2** 6mm pearls after 25 seconds in mauve
- **2** 4mm of deepest mauve pearls
- **2** 2-in. (5cm) headpins
- pair of earring wires
- chainnose or crimping pliers
- diagonal wire cutters

Pearls from Elvee Rosenberg, 212.575.0767 elveerosenberg.com

Dream in Color p. 34

Download your own color wheel at BeadStyleMag.com/colorwheel

necklace 20 in. (50cm)
- **45–49** 30mm matte Lucite ruffled petals, cool blue
- **8–10** 30mm matte Lucite ruffled petals, teal
- **10–12** 15mm matte Lucite ruffled petals, light teal
- 1 gram 8º seed beads, lavender, glossy
- 2 gram 11º seed beads, blue, matte
- flexible beading wire, .014 or .015
- **2** twisted crimps
- toggle clasp
- chainnose and roundnose pliers
- diagonal wire cutters

earrings
- **2** 30mm matte Lucite ruffled petals, cool blue
- **2** 15mm matte Lucite ruffled petals, light teal
- **2** 8mm triangular jump rings
- pair of earring wires
- **2** pairs of chainnose pliers or chainnose and roundnose pliers
- diagonal wire cutters

Easy Stash Fashion p. 38

necklace 18 in. (46cm)
- **15–20** 6–20mm beads
- 25 in. (64cm) large-link textured chain
- **2** 8mm jump rings
- **10–12** 2-in. (5cm) headpins
- lobster claw clasp
- chainnose and roundnose pliers
- diagonal wire cutters

earrings
- **4** 6–8mm beads
- **2** matching links from chain
- **2** 2-in. (5cm) headpins
- pair of earring wires
- chainnose and roundnose pliers
- diagonal wire cutters

Keep Cost Down, Flexibility High p. 40

bracelet
- 2 grams of 11º seed beads in assorted colors
- 64–70 in. (1.2–1.8m) 22–24-gauge wire (I used mostly bits from my scrap bin)
- 11–12 in. (28–30cm) cable chain, 2mm links
- 2 in. (5cm) cable chain, 5mm links
- **2** 4mm jump rings
- 2-in. (5cm) headpin
- lobster claw clasp
- chainnose and roundnose pliers
- diagonal wire cutters
- nylon-jaw pliers (optional)
- graph paper (optional)
- colored pencils or markers (optional)

earrings
- **18** 11º seed beads in assorted colors
- 2 in. (5cm) cable chain, 2mm links
- **2** 2-in. (5cm) headpins
- pair of earring wires
- chainnose and roundnose pliers
- diagonal wire cutters

Not Just for Kids p. 42

bracelet
- **3** sheets of letter-size paper, in three colors
- 16mm butterfly charm
- 2 in. (5cm) chain
- **2** 12mm jump rings
- lobster claw clasp
- scissors
- ruler
- **2** pairs of pliers
- hole-punch pliers
- Vintaj patina, marina
- Vintaj sealant
- Vintaj buffer

earrings
- **2** 16mm butterfly charms
- **2** 7mm jump rings
- pair of earring wires
- **2** pairs of pliers
- Vintaj patina, in marina
- Vintaj sealant
- Vintaj buffer

Fine Facets p. 46

necklace 18 in. (46cm)
- **15** 4mm gemstone rondelles
- 18 in. (46cm) cable chain, 2mm links
- 4mm soldered jump ring
- **15** 2-in. (5cm) 26-gauge headpins
- lobster claw clasp
- chainnose and roundnose pliers
- diagonal wire cutters

earrings
- **10** 4mm gemstone rondelles
- 1 in. (2.5cm) cable chain, 2mm links
- **10** 2-in. (5cm) 26-gauge headpins
- pair of earring wires
- chainnose and roundnose pliers
- diagonal wire cutters

Nurture a Natural Wonder p. 48

necklace 18 in. (46cm)
- 38–40mm river stone pendant
- **4** 26–30mm river stone pendants
- 18 in. (46cm) large-link chain
- **6** 10mm jump rings
- lobster claw clasp
- two pairs of pliers
- Swellegant copper metal coating
- Swellegant verdigris patina
- Swellegant clear sealant
- soft bristle paintbrush
- steel wool (optional)

earrings
- **2** 12mm center-drilled river stones
- **2** 10mm jump rings
- pair of earring wires
- two pairs of pliers
- Swellegant copper metal coating
- Swellegant verdigris patina
- Swellegant clear sealant
- soft bristle paintbrush
- steel wool (optional)

Suitable for Stringing p. 50

necklace 18 in. (46cm)
- 36mm focal bead (Lisa Kan, lisakan.com)
- 2 grams 11º seed beads
- **54–60** fire-polished 6mm rondelles, color A
- **14–20** fire-polished 6mm rondelles, color B
- **16–22** fire-polished 4mm rondelles, color C
- flexible beading wire, .014 or .015
- **2** crimp beads
- toggle clasp
- chainnose or crimping pliers
- diagonal wire cutters

earrings
- **8** fire-polished 6mm rondelles, color A
- **2** fire-polished 6mm rondelles, color B
- **4** fire-polished 4mm rondelles, color C
- **2** 2-in. (5cm) eyepins
- pair of earring wires
- chainnose and roundnose pliers
- diagonal wire cutters

Charm to Spare p. 52

necklace 15–18 in. (36–46cm)
- **5** 14–18mm charms
- **4** 12–24mm gemstone nuggets
- 45–47 in. (1.1–1.2m) chain, 4–6mm links
- **7–9** 6mm jump rings
- **4** 2-in. (5cm) headpins
- toggle clasp
- chainnose and roundnose pliers
- diagonal wire cutters
- Chain Sta Stabilizing Solution (optional)

earrings
- **4** 12–24mm gemstone nuggets
- 8 in. (20cm) chain, 4–6mm inks
- **2** 2-in. (5cm) headpins
- **2** 2-in. (5cm) eyepins
- pair of earring wires
- chainnose and roundnose pliers
- diagonal wire cutters

Lighten Up p. 54

bracelet
- **6** 5-in. (13cm) strands of Lucite calla lilies in several colors
- bracelet-diameter memory wire
- **30** 4mm nugget spacers
- roundnose pliers
- heavy-duty wire cutters or chainnose pliers

earrings
- **2** Lucite calla lilies
- **8** 4mm nugget spacers
- **2** 3-in. (7.6cm) headpins
- pair of earring wires
- chainnose and roundnose pliers
- diagonal wire cutters

I'll Take Bicones with Everything p. 56

necklace 17 in. (43cm)
- 8mm bicone pendant, crystal metallic light gold AB2X
- **24** 4mm bicones, crystal metallic light gold AB2X , color A
- **74–84** 4mm bicones, amethyst, color B
- **36** 4mm bicones, amethyst satin, color C
- **36** 4mm bicones, amethyst AB, color D
- flexible beading wire, .010 or .012
- **2** crimp beads
- toggle clasp
- chainnose or crimping pliers
- diagonal wire cutters

earrings
- **2** 8mm bicone pendant, amethyst (color B)
- **2** 4mm bicones, crystal metallic light gold AB2X (color A)
- **2** 4mm bicones, amethyst satin (color C)
- **2** 4mm bicones, amethyst AB (color D)
- 2-in. (5cm) headpin
- **2** 2-in. (5cm) eyepins
- pair of cup earring posts with backs
- chainnose and roundnose pliers
- diagonal wire cutters
- two-part epoxy
- sponge or eraser

Embrace Chain p. 58

necklace 19 in. (48cm)
- 19 in. (48cm) long-and-short-link chain, 6mm and 4mm links
- 2-in. (5cm) piece of novelty chain
- **28–32** ½-2-in. (1.3–5cm) pieces of chain in different styles and finishes
- lobster claw clasp
- **2** pairs of pliers
- diagonal wire cutters
- **29–33** jump rings (optional)

earrings
- 2½ in. (6.4cm) long-and-short-link chain, 6mm and 4mm links
- 5-in. (13cm) piece of chain small links, type A
- 2-in. (5cm) piece of chain, small links, type B
- pair of earring wires
- **12** jump rings (optional)

Blue-Ribbon Style p. 60

bracelet
- 40 in. (1m) silk ribbon
- 15–20mm button
- **3–4** 15–20mm charms
- 24–30 in. (61–76cm) 24-gauge wire, half-hard
- **3–4** jump rings or headpins and accent beads, depending on the types of charms
- **2** paper clips
- chainnose and roundnose pliers
- diagonal wire cutters

earrings
- **2** 10mm pewter lentil beads
- **2** key and lock charms
- ½ in. (1.3cm) cable chain, 3–4mm links
- **2** 2-in. (5cm) eyepins
- pair of earring wires
- chainnose and roundnose plies
- diagonal wire cutters

Fashion Favors the Bold p. 62

necklace 19½ in. (49.5cm)
- 5 46mm heart slabs
- **2** 8-in (20cm) strands of 15–20mm howlite nuggets
- **2** 6mm round beads
- **2** 4mm round beads
- flexible beading wire, .020 or .021
- **2** 8mm jump rings
- **2** crimp beads
- toggle clasp
- chainnose or crimping pliers
- diagonal wire cutters

earrings
- **2** 15mm howlite nuggets
- **2** 6mm round beads
- **2** 2-in. (5cm) headpins
- pair of earring wires
- chainnose and roundnose pliers
- diagonal wire cutters

Playing It Cool: Mix Silver Textures and Tones p. 64

necklace 25 in. (64cm)
- **25–25** 12–22mm silver and/or silver-toned beads in assorted shapes
- **2** 15–18mm Hill Tribes silver beads
- **2** 12mm cool blue beads
- **20–30** 9–12mm chain links
- **2** figure-8 links
- flexible beading wire, .014 or .015
- **2** crimp beads
- **2** crimp covers
- toggle clasp
- chainnose or crimping pliers
- diagonal wire cutters

earrings
- **2** 12mm textured silver beads
- **2** 2-in. (5cm) headpins
- pair of earring wires
- chainnose and roundnose pliers
- diagonal wire cutters

Gold Standard p. 66

necklace 20 in. (51cm)
- **3** 8-in. (20cm) strands 8mm coin beads
- 16–18 in. (41–46cm) oblong chain, 20mm links
- **9** in. (23cm) 22-gauge wire, half-hard
- flexible beading wire, .014 or .015
- **2** crimp beads
- lobster claw clasp
- chainnose and roundnose pliers
- diagonal wire cutters
- 8mm jump ring (optional)

earrings
- **6** 8mm coin beads
- **2** links oblong chain, 20mm links
- **6** 2-in. (5cm) headpins
- pair of earring wires
- chainnose and roundnose pliers
- diagonal wire cutters

Mining for the Right Copper Mix p. 68

necklace 19 in. (48cm)
- **2** 23mm carved beads
- **5** 12mm lampworked glass beads
- 8-in. (20cm) strand of 5x7mm faceted briolettes
- 2 grams 11º seed beads
- **10** 4mm daisy spacers
- 13-in. (33cm) piece of peanut chain, 6mm links
- flexible beading wire, .014 or .015
- **2** crimp beads
- toggle clasp
- chainnose and roundnose pliers
- diagonal wire cutters

earrings
- **4** 5x7mm faceted briolettes
- **26** 11º seed beads
- 2-in. (5cm) piece of peanut chain, 6mm links
- flexible beading wire, .014 or .015
- **2** crimp beads
- **2** crimp covers
- pair of earring wires
- chainnose and roundnose pliers
- diagonal wire cutters

Clear and Present Style p. 70

patterned-chain necklace 23 in. (58cm)
- **7** 20–24mm rough-cut clear quartz beads
- **6** 12mm clear round beads
- **8** 10mm clear oval beads
- 22 in. (56cm) patterned chain, 8mm links
- **21** 2-in. (5cm) headpins
- 1½-in. (3.8cm) lobster claw clasp
- chainnose and roundnose pliers
- diagonal wire cutters

patterned-chain earrings
- **2** 20–24mm rough-cut clear quartz beads
- **4** links patterned chain, 8mm links
- **2** 2-in. (5cm) headpins
- pair of earring wires
- chainnose and roundnose pliers
- diagonal wire cutters

silver-chain necklace 20½ in. (52.1cm)
- **7** 20–24mm rough-cut clear quartz beads
- **6** 12mm clear round beads
- **8** 10mm clear oval beads
- 21 in. (53cm) silver chain, 4mm links
- **2** 7mm jump rings
- **21** 2-in. (5cm) headpins
- lobster claw clasp
- chainnose and roundnose pliers
- diagonal wire cutters

Take a (Short) Walk on the Wild Side p. 72

carved wood necklace 18 in. (46cm)
- **3** 16mm carved wood beads
- **6** 13mm glass pearls
- **18** 11mm glass pearls
- **2** 9mm glass pearls
- **28** 6mm flat spacer beads
- flexible beading wire, .014 or .015
- **2** crimp beads
- **2** crimp covers
- toggle clasp
- chainnose or crimping pliers
- diagonal wire cutters

carved wood earrings
- **2** 16mm carved wood beads
- **2** 9mm glass pearls
- **2** 6mm flat spacer beads
- **2** 2-in. (5cm) decorative headpins
- pair of earring wires
- chainnose and roundnose pliers
- diagonal wire cutters

recycled glass necklace 17 in. (43cm)
- **3** 10mm top-drilled potato pearls
- **44** 8mm recycled glass beads
- **4** 5mm round beads
- **45–50** 3mm round beads
- flexible beading wire, .014 or .015
- 2 in. (5cm) chain, 6mm links
- 1½-in. (3.8cm) headpin
- **2** crimp beads
- lobster claw clasp
- chainnose or crimping pliers
- diagonal wire cutters

Find Your Balance p. 74

fish necklace 20 in. (51cm)
- 65mm Hill Tribes silver fish bead
- 16-in. (41cm) strand 13mm tumbled quartz nuggets
- **8–10** 4mm apatite rondelles
- **18–20** 4mm aquamarine rondelles
- flexible beading wire, .014 and .015
- **2** crimp beads
- box clasp
- chainnose or crimping pliers
- diagonal wire cutters

fish earrings
- **2** 20mm Hill Tribes silver fish beads
- **2** 9mm tumbled quartz nuggets
- **2** 7mm pinch beads
- 5 in. chain, 2–4mm links
- **4** 2-in. (5cm) headpins
- pair of earring wires
- chainnose and roundnose pliers
- diagonal wire cutters

druzy necklace 18½ in. (47cm)
- 50mm top-drilled chalcedony druzy bead
- **7** 22mm tumbled quartz nuggets
- 16-in. (41cm) 8mm tumbled quartz nuggets, top-drilled
- 4mm turquoise rondelle
- flexible beading wire, .014 and .015
- **2** crimp beads
- toggle clasp
- chainnose or crimping pliers
- diagonal wire cutters

Refresh Your Memory Wire p. 78

bracelet
- **18** 10mm round beads
- 1 gram 11º seed beads
- **2** coils bracelet-diameter memory wire
- 24 in. (61cm) 24-gauge wire, dead-soft
- heavy-duty wire cutters
- two-part epoxy

earrings
- **2** 10mm round beads
- **4** 11º seed beads
- **2** coils bracelet-diameter memory wire
- heavy-duty wire cutters
- two-part epoxy
- metal file or emery board

Resources

I buy most of my beads at my local bead shops, Michaels, JoAnn's, and bead shows like the Bead&Button Show. Here are some of my favorites that I look for at shows and online.

Bead Palace
beadpalaceinc.com

Dakota Stones
dakotastones.com

Beadin' Path
beadinpath.com

Fire Mountain Gems and Beads
firemountaingems.com

Fusion Beads
fusionbeads.com

Green Girl Studios
greengirlstudios.com

Kabela Design
kabeladesign.com

Nina Designs
ninadesigns.com

Saki Silver
sakisilver.com

Silk Painting Is Fun
silkpaintingisfun.com

Swellegant
cforiginals.net

Tierracast
tierracast.com

Via Murano
viamurano.com

Vintaj
vintaj.com

Find projects, how-to videos, tips, and more at BeadStyleMag.com. Don't forget to register (it's fast and free!) for even more goodies.

Techniques Review

wrapped loop

1 Make sure you have at least 1¼ in. (3.2cm) of wire above the bead. With the tip of your chainnose pliers, grasp the wire directly above the bead. Bend the wire (above the pliers) into a right angle.
2 Using roundnose pliers, position the jaws in the bend.
3 Bring the wire over the top jaw of the roundnose pliers.
4 Reposition the pliers' lower jaw snugly into the loop. Curve the wire downward around the roundnose pliers. *This is the first half of a wrapped loop.*
5 Grasp the loop with chainnose pliers.
6 Wrap the wire tall around the wire stem, covering the stem between the loop and the top bead. Trim the excess wrapping wire and press the end close to the stem.

plain loop

1 Trim the wire ⅜ in. (1cm) above the top of the bead. Make a right-angle bend close to the bead.
2 Grab the wire's tip with roundnose pliers. Roll the wire to form a half circle.
3 Reposition the pliers in the loop and continue rolling, forming a centered circle above the bead.
4 The finished loop should look like this.

flattened crimp

1 Hold a crimp bead with the tip of your chainnose pliers. Squeeze the pliers firmly to flatten the crimp bead. Tug the clasp to make sure the crimp has a solid grip on the wire. If the wire slides, remove the flattened crimp bead and repeat with a new crimp bead.
2 The flattened crimp bead should look like this.

folded crimp

1 Position the crimp bead in the notch closest to the crimping pliers' handle.
2 Separate the wires and firmly squeeze the crimp bead.
3 Move the partially indented crimp bead into the notch at the pliers' tip. Squeeze the pliers, folding the bead in half at the indentation.
4 The folded crimp bead should look like this.

open a jump ring, loop, or link

1 Hold the jump ring, loop, or link with chainnose and roundnose pliers or two pairs of chainnose or bentnose pliers.
2 To open the jump ring or loop, bring one pair of pliers toward you. Reverse the action to close.

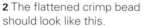
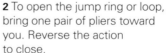

crimp cover

Place a crimp cover over a folded or flattened crimp. Use crimping pliers to gently squeeze the cover together until it resembles a bead.

measure and cut flexible beading wire

Decide how long you want your necklace to be. Add 6 in. (15cm) and cut a piece of beading wire to that length. (For a bracelet, add 5 in./13cm.)

wraps above a top–drilled bead

1 Center a top-drilled bead on a 3-in. (7.6cm) piece of wire. Bend each wire upward to form a squared-off U shape.
2 Cross the wires into an X above the bead.
3 Using chainnose pliers, make a small bend in each wire so the ends form a right angle.
4 Wrap the horizontal wire around the vertical wire as in a wrapped loop. Trim the excess wire.

make a coil

1 Grasp the end of a wire with roundnose pliers, and rotate the pliers to form a small loop.
2 Grasp across the loop with chainnose or flatnose pliers, and use your fingers to guide the wire tail around the loop. Leaving space between the rotations makes a loose spiral; leaving no space makes a tight spiral. Continue rotating until the spiral is the desired size.
3 With chainnose pliers, make a bend above the spiral.

attach a clasp

1 On one end of the piece, string a spacer, a crimp bead, a spacer, and a clasp or clasp half. Go back through the last few beads strung and tighten the wire.

2 On the other end of the piece, repeat step 1 with the other clasp half, or substitute a 3–4-in. (7.6–10cm) piece of chain if desired. Check the fit; add or remove beads if needed. On each end, crimp the crimp bead and trim the excess wire. Close a crimp cover over each crimp, if desired.

gilding metal or adding patina

1 Rub a small amount of patina onto a charm.
2 Rub lightly with buffer and apply sealer. Let dry.

half-hitch knot

Pass the needle under the thread between two beads. A loop will form as you pull the thread through. Cross over the thread between the beads, sew through the loop, and pull gently to draw the knot into the beadwork.

Acknowledgments

This book is dedicated to my family and friends, who are always relentlessly supportive of my adventures—beady and otherwise. I'd also like to thank my *Bead Style* family—past and present—especially Naomi Fujimoto, Jane Konkel, Kelsey Lawler, and all the contributors to the magazine who have shared their talents. I would also like to thank Karin Van Voorhees and Lisa Bergman, who made this book a pleasure to create.

About the Author

Originally from the Chicago area, Cathy Jakicic moved to Milwaukee to attend Marquette University in the early '80s and never left. She began making jewelry in the wee hours of the morning while working the late shift at a Milwaukee daily newspaper right after college.

In 2005, she landed her dream job as editor of *Bead Style* magazine. Since she started, she has seen the magazine grow from a print-only operation to include a vibrant website and digital offerings, with the love of beads always at the core of everything.

Even after decades of beading, Cathy still enjoys learning new skills at the annual Bead&Button Show in Milwaukee, and occasionally finds the time to sell her jewelry. She frequently donates her beaded work to nonprofit organizations—primarily those that support the arts as well as the health and welfare of women and families.

In addition to making jewelry, Cathy enjoys travel, baking, gardening, movies, books, and spending time with friends and family. She lives in a beautiful, old house in Milwaukee that's filled with beads, dust, carved wood, and leaded glass.

Index

Here's the inside track to more incredible projects!

The perfect ingredients for inspiration! Combine 26 well-known jewelry designers, mix in a creative challenge, swap leftover bead collections, and what do you get? Thirty-two savory projects and a foolproof recipe for jewelry success!
64421 • $19.95

Improve your skills with every project when you follow the step-by-step photos and clear instructions in this friendly guide. Master easy techniques including crimping, connecting, and finishing, plus discover how to work with unusual stringing materials.
62991 • $21.95

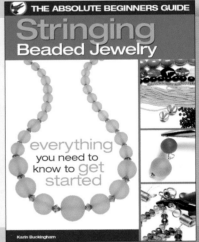

Jump-start your creativity with inspiration from lush woodlands, playful gardens, and tranquil seas. Learn how to balance color, texture, and scale as you create 30 projects that integrate chain, wire, crystals, seed beads, and gorgeous art beads.
64285 • $19.95